INTRODUCTION

This bibliography attempts to cover all the published works in English by or about Philip K. Dick. An attempt has been made to include information on `foreign language' items, but the coverage of these, and of English language items published outside of the United Kingdom or the United States, is rather sparse due to the lack of adequate reference sources.

An attempt has been made to be as `complete' as possible, and all items of possible relevance have been included, no matter how `minor'. However, there are bound to be many secondary items (particularly in fanzines) that have been omitted. These omissions will hopefully be corrected in future editions of this bibliography.

The bibliography is divided into eighteen sections, as follows:

Awards and Pseudonyms

This section describes any awards that the author has won, and any pseudonyms that he wrote under.

A. Stories

This section contains all pieces of fiction (excluding poetry) that appeared as part of a larger publication (e.g. a magazine or a collection). Entries for each item are in chronological order although, generally, no attempt is made to identify the month in which an anthology or collection first appeared. If an item appeared under multiple different titles, then all appearances are listed under the most common title, with variant titles mentioned explicitly and with cross-references from all such variant titles.

Only the first printing of anthologies and collections is given, unless a reprint was under a different title or had differing contents, in which case all such variants are listed. Conversely, all magazine appearances are given, except where the same magazine was published in the same month in several different countries.

Where the story was originally submitted under a different title, this title is given in brackets after the story name.

The approximate length of each item is identified by an abbreviation of the form (tt) or (tt-n) after the story title, where `tt' is one of:

    sss - Short Short Story or Vignette
    ss - Short Story
    NT - Novelette
    NA - Novella
    SN - Short Novel
    N   - Novel

and `-n', if specified, indicates that the item was serialized in `n' parts. These categories are generally taken from the category under which the item was originally published, rather than representing a definite word limit.

B. Books

This section contains all pieces of fiction (excluding poetry) that were published separately, even if this consisted of only a pamphlet or similar. Entries for each item are in chronological order of first publication by a given publisher (or publisher's imprint). Reprints and re-issues under the same imprint are collected together, in chronological order, under a single entry heading for convenience.

Where the book was originally submitted under a different title, this title is given in brackets after the book name.

Each entry is of the basic format:

    Publisher (type) ISBN, Date, Pagination, Price (Artist)

although some items will be excluded from certain entries as described below. The Publisher listed is the imprint given on the book and applies to all other entries under the current heading. Publishers who have published the same book under multiple imprints will have separate entries for each imprint.

The type field identifies the category of book and may be `hb' for hardback books, `pb' for "rack-size" paperbacks, `tp' for paperbacks that are larger than "rack-size" and `ph' for pamphlets that have no form of binding at all. Any other types will be specified explicitly.

Where possible the last two groups of the ISBN for the book (book number and check digit) are given as these should uniquely identify the edition in question (although not all publishers follow the rules). If an ISBN is not available, the book number allocated by the publisher is used or, failing that, the Library of Congress or British Library Catalogue Number. For DAW Books, the "collector's number" is also given in brackets after the ISBN. Reprints with no ISBN (or equivalent) listed share the same ISBN as the previous edition listed.

The date given represents the official publication date for the book - it should be borne in mind that most US publishers ship books to the bookshops a month before the official date (a practice that is much less frequent in the UK). Reprints that have only a date listed imply that no other changes occurred to the book as part of this printing.

The pagination given corresponds to the highest-numbered page in the book, excluding any trailing material not directly relevant (e.g. advertisements or biographical sketches). If the item does not have page numbers, or the page numbers are not consecutive (e.g. in an omnibus where each included `book' starts at page 1) then the pagination represents a count of the pages in the book.

The price represents the price given on the book, where possible, or the `published price' if no price is marked. Books published in the UK will be priced in `old money' (e.g. 25/-, 3/6d) for editions prior to 15/2/71, and in `new money' (e.g. £3.50, 75p) for editions after that date. Australian and Canadian prices are indicated by prefixing the price with `A' or `C' (e.g. A$3.50, C$2.00). All other prices should, hopefully, be self-explanatory.

The cover artist is listed where credited or where known. An entry of "(?)" indicates that the artist could not be identified or that the edition in question has not been seen. If this item is omitted completely for an edition, and some item other than just the date HAS been specified, then it implies that there was no artwork on the cover.

In some cases an additional item may be listed giving the `number' of the edition (e.g. (12th), (52nd)) as indicated in the book itself. It should be borne in mind that such numbering is frequently inaccurate.

C. Series

This section lists all items that are known to form part of a series or which have one or more characters or locations in common. The section omits any stories that are collected in the books that are listed as part of the same entry. Where possible, entries are given in internal chronological order.

D. Poems, Songs, Plays and TV/Film Scripts

This section lists all poetry, songs, plays, film or TV scripts, or any similar material that was formally published as part of a larger publication (e.g. a magazine or a collection). The format is the same as for section A. If a poem or song does not have a formal title then the first line is listed, in quotation marks.

E. Poem, Song, Play & TV/Film Script Volumes

This section contains all items or collections of poetry, songs, plays, film or TV scripts, or similar, that were published separately, even if this consisted of only a pamphlet or other ephemeral publication. The format is the same as for section B.

F. Articles

This section contains all major pieces of non-fiction by the author that appeared as part of a larger publication (e.g. a magazine or a collection). Typically this will mean all items that have been given a formal title by the author (or publisher). The format is the same as for section A except that formal titles, where given, are put in quotation marks (e.g. "A Major Article"). Items not in quotation marks correspond to a description of the item in question (e.g. Speech on Science Fiction).

G. Miscellaneous

This section contains all minor pieces of non-fiction by the author that appeared as part of a larger publication (such as introductions to books) as well as odd items that do not fit elsewhere. In particular, any interviews conducted with the author are held in this section. The format is the same as for section F, except that all interviews are listed under "Interview", in alphabetical order of interviewer.

H. Non-Fiction Books

This section contains all collections or items of non-fiction that were published separately, even if this consisted of only a pamphlet or similar. The format is the same as for section B.

I. Edited Books

This section contains all items that were edited by the author, including, where known, any magazines or fanzines for which the author was editor. The format is the same as for section B.

J. Other Media

This section lists all known films, records, TV, radio or comic strip adaptations, either by the author, or based on material by the author. This section cannot be regarded as definitive as reference material in this area is still very sparse. Entries in this section are listed in alphabetical order of title, with details given, where appropriate, of the item in section A or B on which the material is based. Items based on books are listed in capital letters; items based on stories in mixed upper and lower case.

K. Articles on the Author

This section contains all known articles that relate to the author or his work, excluding book reviews, that appeared as part of a larger publication (e.g. a magazine or a collection). The format is the same as for section F, except that entries are in alphabetical order of author, with multiple articles by the same author being arranged in alphabetical order of title. Any articles for which the author is not known are listed at the beginning of the section in alphabetical order of title.

L. Reviews

This section contains all known reviews of books by, or edited by, the author. Entries for books that have appeared under multiple titles are listed under the most common title. Within each entry, items are listed in alphabetical order of the publication within which the review appeared.

M. Books about the Author

This section contains all collections or items about the author that were published separately, even if this consisted of only a pamphlet or similar. The format is the same as for section B, except that entries are listed in alphabetical order of the author or editor of the work in question.

N. Phantom and Forthcoming Titles

This section attempts to list all titles, or editions, that have been announced or listed at some point but which have not yet been published, or were published under a different name, or were cancelled or were falsely attributed to the author. The entries are in alphabetical order of entry, and each entry contains a note explaining the origin of the item.

O. Related Works by Other Authors

This section contains any books or stories by other authors that are related to the author in question, either because they share characters or locations with books by that author, or because they refer indirectly to the author or his writing, or because they are contained in a collection of the author's work. Entries are in alphabetical order of author, with multiple entries by the same author in alphabetical order of title. The format of each entry is the same as in sections A and B, depending on whether the item is a `story' or a `book'.

P. Textual Variations

This section contains information on any major textual variations that are known. Simple variations (such as a story being expanded into a novel, or a book being revised from one edition to the next) do not usually warrant an entry here and are mentioned in the body of the text.

Q. Chronological Listing of Fiction

This section contains a chronological listing, by year, of all
the items contained in sections A and B. Where known, this
ordering is based on the date that the item was originally
submitted through Dick's agent. Within each year an attempt is
made to order items by the month in which they appeared, or were,
submitted, with items for which the month of publication is
unknown placed at the end of the entries for the year.

A Note on Alphabetical Ordering

In all the sections that are ordered alphabetically, the ordering
is done by ignoring the difference between upper and lower case,
ignoring any leading definite or indefinite article and by
ignoring all punctuation (such as spaces and apostrophes). Thus a
sample ordering might contain:

    Ike and the Puppet
    "I Killed Him Yesterday"
    I'll Go Home Again
    The Illuminated Manuscript
    I Love Her Madly

Entries for which the first `word' is a number are listed as if
the number were spelt out (e.g. `45 Ways to Murder' is listed
under `Forty-Five').

A Note on Dates

All dates, where relevant, are in UK format (Day-Month-Year).

ACKNOWLEDGEMENTS

As with every bibliographer before us, we must acknowledge our debt to the standard reference books, both inside and outside the field without which this bibliography would not have been possible. In particular, the following reference sources were consulted:

Ashley, Mike: THE CRYPTOPHILE: Cryptic Publications, 1988
Bishop, Gerald: SCIENCE FICTION BOOKS PUBLISHED IN BRITAIN 1970
    & 1971, 1972 & 1973, 1974 - 1978, 1/82 - 10/83: Aardvark House,
    1970 - 1984
Bleiler, Richard: THE INDEX TO ADVENTURE MAGAZINE: Starmont, 1990
Boyajian, Jerry & Kenneth R Johnson: INDEX TO THE SCIENCE FICTION
    MAGAZINES 1977, 1978, 1979, 1980, 1981, 1982, 1983, 1984: TWACI
    Press, 1981 - 1985
Boyajian, Jerry & Kenneth R Johnson: INDEX TO THE SEMI-PROFESSIONAL
    FANTASY MAGAZINES 1982, 1983: TWACI Press, 1983 - 1984
Brown, Charles N & Bill Contento: SCIENCE FICTION, FANTASY & HORROR
    IN PRINT: 1984, 1985, 1986, 1987, 1988, 1989, 1990, 1991:
    Locus Press, 1986 - 1992
Burger, Joanne: SF PUBLISHED IN 1970, 1971, 1972, 1977: Burger,
    1971 - 1974, 1979
Burgess, Michael: REFERENCE GUIDE TO SCIENCE FICTION, FANTASY AND
    HORROR: Libraries Unlimited, 1992
Chalker, Jack L. & Mark Owings: THE SCIENCE-FANTASY PUBLISHERS:
    Mirage, 1991
Contento, William & Martin H. Greenberg: INDEX TO CRIME AND
    MYSTERY ANTHOLOGIES: G.K. Hall, 1990
Contento, William: INDEX TO SCIENCE FICTION ANTHOLOGIES AND
    COLLECTIONS and ditto 1977 - 1983: G.K. Hall, 1978 & 1984
Cook, Dorothy E & Estelle A Fidell et al.: SHORT STORY INDEX
    - 1949, 1950 - 1954, 1955 - 1958, 1959 - 1963, 1964 - 1968,
    1969 - 1973, 1974 - 1978, 1979 - 1983, 1984 - 1988, 1989:
    H.W. Wilson, 1953 - 1990
Cook, Michael L: MONTHLY MURDERS: Greenwood Press, 1982
Cook, Michael L. & Steve Miller: MYSTERY, DETECTIVE AND ESPIONAGE
    FICTION: Greenwood Press, 1988
Cook, Michael L.: MYSTERY FANFARE: Bowling Green, 1983
Corrick, James A.: DOUBLE YOUR PLEASURE: THE ACE SF DOUBLE,
    Gryphon Books, 1989
Covell, Ian: INDEX TO DAW BOOKS, Galactic Central, 1989
Currey, L.W.: SCIENCE FICTION AND FANTASY AUTHORS: A BIBLIOGRAPHY
    OF FIRST PRINTINGS OF THEIR FICTION: G.K. Hall, 1979
Day, Donald B: INDEX TO THE SCIENCE FICTION MAGAZINES 1926 - 1950:
    Perri Press, 1952
Delmas, Henri & Alain Julian: LE RAYON SF: Editions Milan, 1983
DeVore, Howard & Donald Franson: A HISTORY OF THE HUGO, NEBULA AND
    INTERNATIONAL FANTASY AWARDS: Misfit Press, 1978
Diviney, Jim & Sheila: INDEX TO ASTOUNDING: BRITISH EDITION:
    NOV 53 - AUG 63
Goimard, Jacques: L'ANNÉE 1977-1978 DE LA SCIENCE FICTION ET DU
    FANTASTIQUE & ditto 1978-1979 & ditto 1979-1980 & ditto 1980-1981:
    Juillard, 1978 - 1981

Hall, H.W.: SCIENCE FICTION BOOK REVIEW INDEX, 1923 - 1973 and
    ditto 1974 - 1979 and ditto 1980 - 1984: Gale, 1974 - 1985
Hall, H.W.: SCIENCE FICTION AND FANTASY REFERENCE INDEX,
    1878 - 1985: Gale Research, 1987
Hassón, Moisés: INDEX TO MEXICAN SCIENCE FICTION MAGAZINES:
    Hassón, 1991
James, Edward: INDEX TO FOUNDATION 1-40: Science Fiction
    Foundation, 1988
Johansen, Klaus & Henry Madsen: SCIENCE FICTION BIBLIOGRAFI 1741 -
    1989: Science Fiction Kredsen, 1992
Johansen, Klaus: SCIENCE FICTION BIBLIOGRAFI 1741 - 1989: TILL ÆG OG
    RETTELSER 1990-1991: Science Fiction Kredsen, 1991
Johansen, Klaus: SCIENCE FICTION NOVELLEREGISTER: Science Fiction
    Kredsen, 1991
Metcalf, Norm: THE INDEX OF SCIENCE FICTION MAGAZINES
    1951 - 1965: J. Ben Stark, 1968
NESFA: INDEX TO THE SCIENCE FICTION MAGAZINES (AND ORIGINAL
    ANTHOLOGIES), 1966 - 1970, 1971 - 1972, 1973, 1974, 1975,
    1976, 1977 - 1978, 1979 - 1980, 1981, 1982, 1983: NESFA,
    1971 - 1984
Parnell, Frank & Mike Ashley: MONTHLY TERRORS: Greenwood Press,
    1985
Pattison, Jim: CHEAP STREET: A PRELIMINARY BIBLIOGRAPHY:
    Galactic Central, 1990
Reginald, R: SCIENCE FICTION AND FANTASY LITERATURE: 1700 - 1974
    & ditto 1975 - 1991: Gale Research, 1979, 1992
Riche, Daniel: L'ANNÉE 1982-1983 DE LA SCIENCE FICTION ET DU
    FANTASTIQUE: Temps Future, 1983
Robbins, Leonard A.: THE PULP MAGAZINE INDEX, FIRST SERIES &
    SECOND SERIES & THIRD SERIES: Starmont House, 1989 - 1990
Robinson, Roger: WHO'S HUGH: Beccon, 1987
Smith, Curtis C: TWENTIETH-CENTURY SCIENCE-FICTION WRITERS,
    SECOND EDITION: Macmillan, 1986
Stephens, Christopher P.: A CHECKLIST OF PHANTASIA PRESS:
    Ultramarine Press. 1991
Stephens, Christopher P.: A CHECKLIST OF ULTRAMARINE PRESS:
    Ultramarine Press. 1991
Stone, Graham: AUSTRALIAN SCIENCE FICTION INDEX: 1925 - 1967 &
    ditto 1968 - 1975: Australian SF Association, 1968 & 1976
Stone, Graham: INDEX TO THE BRITISH SCIENCE FICTION MAGAZINES
    VOLS 1 - 3: Australian SF Association, 1977 - 1979
Tuck, Donald H: THE ENCYCLOPAEDIA OF SCIENCE FICTION AND FANTASY,
    VOLUMES 1 - 3: Advent, 1974, 1978, 1982
Tymn, Marshall & Michael Ashley: SCIENCE FICTION, FANTASY AND
    WEIRD FICTION MAGAZINES: Greenwood, 1985
Vegetti, Ernesto: REPERTORY OF THE ITALIAN PROFESSIONALS IN SCIENCE
    FICTION AND FANTASY: 1981, 1982-1983: World SF - Italy, 1982, 1984
Williams, Richard: THE DRAGONBY BIBLIOGRAPHIES: Dragonby Press,
    1987 - 1991
Williams, Richard: BRITISH PAPERBACK CHECKLISTS: Dragonby Press,
    1984 - 1991
Williams, Richard: BRITISH HARDBACK CHECKLISTS: Dragonby Press,
    1987 - 1990

AMERICAN BOOK PUBLISHING RECORD 1950 - 1977, 1978 - 1987:
   Bowker, 1978 - 1988
BOOKS IN ENGLISH: Cumulation 1971 - 1980, 1981 - 1985
BOOKS IN PRINT
BRITISH BOOKS IN PRINT
BRITISH BOOKS OUT OF PRINT: 1976 - 1985
BRITISH NATIONAL BIBLIOGRAPHY 1950 - 1984: The British Library,
   1955 - 1985
CUMULATIVE BOOK INDEX 1943 - 1986: H.W. Wilson, 1950 - 1987
WHITAKER'S CUMULATIVE BOOK LIST 1948 - 1984: Whitaker, 1953 - 1985

Special thanks also go to Gregg Rickman for graciously allowing
us to include the fruits of his research, particularly as given
in TO THE HIGH CASTLE: PHILIP K. DICK: A LIFE. Thanks also go to
Andrew Butler, Jaak Doom, Harry Gerdts, Horvàth György, Greg Lee,
Steve Sneyd, Jeff Young and Martin Young who provided information
for an earlier edition of this bibliography.

We are always interested in hearing of corrections or updates to
the bibliography, which should be sent to either of us at the
addresses given below.

Phil Stephensen-Payne,   Gordon Benson, Jr.,
`Imladris',   P.O. Box 40494,
25A, Copgrove Road,   ALBUQUERQUE,
LEEDS,   New Mexico 87196,
West Yorkshire,   UNITED STATES OF AMERICA
LS8 2SP,
England.

A Galactic Central Publication

First Edition: July 1986
Second Edition: February 1989
Third Edition: February 1990
Fourth Edition: February 1995

PHILIP KINDRED DICK
(Born: 16-Dec-1928; Chicago, Illinois)
(Died: 2-Mar-1982; Santa Ana, California)

<u>Awards</u>: *1963: HUGO - Best Novel -* THE MAN IN THE HIGH CASTLE
1967: BSFA AWARD - THE THREE STIGMATA OF PALMER ELDRICH
1975: JOHN W. CAMPBELL MEMORIAL AWARD - Best Novel -
FLOW MY TEARS, THE POLICEMAN SAID
1979: GRAOUILLY D'OR - Best Novel - A SCANNER DARKLY
1980: PLAYBOY - Best New Fiction Writer - Frozen Journey
1983: HUGO - Best Dramatic Presentation - BLADE RUNNER
1983: SEIUN TASHO - Best Dramatic Presentation -
BLADE RUNNER
1983: SF CHRONICLE - Best Dramatic Presentation -
BLADE RUNNER
1985: GIGAMESH - Best SF Novel - THE TRANSMIGRATION OF
TIMOTHY ARCHER
1985: KURD LASSWITZ - Best Foreign Novel - VALIS
1987: DAEDALUS - Best SF Novel - RADIO FREE ALBEMUTH
1989: GIGAMESH - Best SF Novel - NOW WAIT FOR LAST YEAR
1989: GIGAMESH - Special Award - PUTTERING ABOUT IN
A SMALL LAND
1989: LAZAR KOMARCIC (Yugoslavia) - Best Foreign SF Novel
- FLOW MY TEARS, THE POLICEMAN SAID
1989: READERCON - Best Re-Issue - VALIS (Kerosina edition)
1990: ALKOR - Best Translated Short Story - The Taste
Beware the Wabe (?)
1990: GIGAMESH - Best SF Collection/Anthology - BEYOND
LIES THE WUB
1990: READERCON - Best Non-Fiction - THE DARK-HAIRED GIRL
1990: TÄHTIVAELTAJA AWARD - A SCANNER DARKLY
1992: TÄHTIVAELTAJA AWARD - THE MAN IN THE HIGH CASTLE

<u>Pseudonyms</u>: Jack Dowland; Chipdip K. Kill (1 fanzine item only);
Richard Phillips; Mark Van Dyke (juvenilia only);
Teddy (juvenilia only - unconfirmed);

A. *Stories*

A1. Adjustment Team (NT)
Orbit SF #4, 9/10-54
THE SANDS OF MARS AND OTHER STORIES, Anon, Jubilee, 1958
THE BOOK OF PHILIP K. DICK / THE TURNING WHEEL (1973)
Galaktika #52, 1983 {translated into Hungarian, as
Helyreigazító Csoport}
SECOND VARIETY (1987) {not in Citadel Twilight edition}
WE CAN REMEMBER IT FOR YOU WHOLESALE (1990)
{Citadel Twilight edition only}

A2. The Alien Mind (ss)
     Yuba City High Times 20-2-81
     Fantasy and Science Fiction 10-81
     THE BEST FROM FANTASY AND SCIENCE FICTION: 24TH SERIES,
          Ferman, Scribner's, 1982
     I HOPE I SHALL ARRIVE SOON (1985)
     THE LITTLE BLACK BOX / THE EYE OF THE SIBYL (1987)
     Magical Blend #17, 10-87
     RACCONTI DI FANTASCIENZA, Torchio, Breschia, 1990
          {translated into Italian, as La Mente Aliena}
     WE CAN REMEMBER IT FOR YOU WHOLSESALE (1991) {Grafton
          edition only}

A3. A. Lincoln, Simulacrum (N-2)
     Amazing 11-69, 1-70 {with 3,000 word ending written
          by Ted White}
     WE CAN BUILD YOU (1972)

A4. All We Marsmen (N-3)
     Worlds of Tomorrow 8, 10, 12-63
     MARTIAN TIME-SLIP (1964) {expanded}
     Galaxie #32, 12-66 & #33, 1-67 & #34, 2-67   {translated
          into French, as Nous Les Martiens}

A5. Autofac (NT)
     Galaxy 11-55; #35, 2-56 (UK);
     THE VARIABLE MAN AND OTHER STORIES (1957) {not in French
          editions}
     THE RUINS OF EARTH, Disch, Putnams, 1971
     BEYOND CONTROL, Silverberg, Nelson, 1972
     SCIENCE FACT/FICTION, Farrell/Gage/Pfordresher/Rodriques,
          Scott, Foresman, 1974
     THE BEST OF PHILIP K. DICK (1977)
     Science Fiction Magasinet #6, 1977/78 {translated into
          Danish, as Autofab}
     ROBOTS, ANDROIDS AND MECHANICAL ODDITIES (1984)
     THE DAYS OF PERKY PAT / THE MINORITY REPORT (1987)

A6. Beyond Lies the Wub (ss)
     Planet Stories 7-52
     Weird Science Illustories #1, 195?
     THE PRESERVING MACHINE AND OTHER STORIES (1969)
     ALPHA 3, Silverberg, Ballantine, 1972
     DE ONMOGELIJKE PLANEET (1976) {translated into Dutch
          by Amos Baat, as Het Goffermaal}
     THE BEST OF PHILIP K. DICK (1977)
     CONSTELLATIONS, Edwards, Gollancz, 1980
     FIRST VOYAGES, Knight/Greenberg/Olander, Avon, 1981
     PETER DAVISON'S BOOK OF ALIEN MONSTERS, Davison,
          Sparrow, 1982
     BEYOND LIES THE WUB / THE SHORT HAPPY LIFE OF THE BROWN
          OXFORD (1987)

A7. Beyond the Door (ss) ["The Cuckoo Clock"]
     Fantastic Universe 1-54
     SECOND VARIETY (1987) {not in Citadel Twilight edition}
     WE CAN REMEMBER IT FOR YOU WHOLESALE (1990)
          {Citadel Twilight edition only}

A8. The Black Box (sss)
     The Berkeley Gazette 16-9-42

A9. Breakfast at Twilight (ss)
     Amazing 7-54; Vol 1 #6, 10-54 (UK);
     Fantastic 11-66
     EEN SWIBBEL VOOR DAG EN NACHT (1969) {translated into
          Dutch by C.A.G. Von Den Broek, as Ontbijt in
          de Schemering}
     THE BOOK OF PHILIP K. DICK / THE TURNING WHEEL (1973)
     THE BEST OF PHILIP K. DICK (1977)
     PHILIP K. DICK OMNIBUS (1977) {translated into Dutch by
          C.A.G. Von Den Broek, as Ontbijt in de Schemering}
     Galaktika #52, 1983 {translated into Hungarian, as
          Reggeli Szürkületkor}
     SECOND VARIETY (1987) {not in Citadel Twilight edition}
     AMAZING SCIENCE FICTION STORIES: THE WILD YEARS 1946-1955,
          Greenberg, TSR, 1987
     WE CAN REMEMBER IT FOR YOU WHOLESALE (1990)
          {Citadel Twilight edition only}

A10. The Builder (ss)
    Amazing 12-53/1-54; Vol 1 #3, 4-54 (UK);
    A HANDFUL OF DARKNESS (1955)
    Amazing 6-67
    EEN HANDVOL DUISTERNIS (1969) {translated into Dutch by
        Henk Bouwman, as De Doe-Het-Zelver}
    PHILIP K. DICK OMNIBUS (1977) {translated into Dutch by
        Henk Bouwman, as De Doe-Het-Zelver}
    BEYOND LIES THE WUB / THE SHORT HAPPY LIFE OF THE BROWN
        OXFORD (1987)

A11. Cadbury, the Beaver Who Lacked (ss)
    privately circulated in early 1970's
    THE LITTLE BLACK BOX / THE EYE OF THE SIBYL (1987)
    WE CAN REMEMBER IT FOR YOU WHOLSESALE (1991) {Grafton
        edition only}

A12. Cantata 140 (SN)
    Fantasy and Science Fiction 7-64
    THE CRACK IN SPACE (1966) {expanded and adapted}

A13. Captive Market (ss)
    If 4-55
    THE FIRST WORLD OF IF, Quinn/Wulff, Quinn, 1957
    THE PRESERVING MACHINE AND OTHER STORIES (1969)
    TOMORROW INC., Greenberg/Olander, Taplinger, 1976
    DE ONMOGELIJKE PLANEET (1976) {translated into Dutch
        by Amos Baat, as Monopolie}
    LES DÉLIRES DIVERGENTS DE PHILIP K. DICK (1979) {translated
        into French by Alain Dorémieux}
    THE DAYS OF PERKY PAT / THE MINORITY REPORT (1987)
    THE GREAT SF STORIES 17 (1955), Asimov/Greenberg, DAW, 1988

A14. Chains of Air, Web of Aether (NT) ["The Man Who Knew How
        to Lose"]
    STELLAR #5, Del Rey, Del Rey, 1980
    THE DIVINE INVASION (1981) {expanded and adapted}
    I HOPE I SHALL ARRIVE SOON (1985)
    THE LITTLE BLACK BOX / THE EYE OF THE SIBYL (1987)
    WE CAN REMEMBER IT FOR YOU WHOLSESALE (1991) {Grafton
        edition only}

A15. The Chromium Fence (ss)
    Imagination 7-55
    THE FATHER-THING (1987)
    SECOND VARIETY (1991) {Citadel Twilight edition only}

A16. Colony (ss)
    Galaxy 6-53; Vol 3 #8, 10-53 (UK);
    A HANDFUL OF DARKNESS (1955)
    [dramatized as J4, 1956]
    EEN HANDVOL DUISTERNIS (1969) {translated into Dutch by
            Henk Bouwman, as De Kolonie}
    SPACE OPERA, Aldiss, Weidenfeld & Nicolson, 1974;
            {not in Orbit edition}
    DE ONMOGELIJKE PLANEET (1976) {translated into Dutch
            by Henk Bouwman, as De Kolonie}
    THE BEST OF PHILIP K. DICK (1977)
    BEYOND LIES THE WUB / THE SHORT HAPPY LIFE OF THE BROWN
            OXFORD (1987)
    ROBERT SILVERBERG'S WORLDS OF WONDER, Silverberg,
            Warner, 1987
    MEMORIA TOTALE (1990) {translated into Italian by
            Maurizio Nati, as Colonia}

A17. The Commuter (ss)
    Amazing 8/9-53; Vol 1 #1, 12-53 (UK);
    Amazing 12-66
    EEN SWIBBEL VOOR DAG EN NACHT (1969) {translated into
            Dutch by C.A.G. Von Den Broek, as De Forens}
    THE BOOK OF PHILIP K. DICK / THE TURNING WHEEL (1973)
    BEYOND TOMORROW, Harding, Wren, 1976; NEL, 1977 (14 of 17)
    PHILIP K. DICK OMNIBUS (1977) {translated into Dutch by
            C.A.G. Von Den Broek, as De Forens}
    LE LIVRE D'OR DE LA SCIENCE-FICTION PHILIP K. DICK (1979)
            {translated into French by Marcel Thaon}
    SECOND VARIETY (1987) {not in Citadel Twilight edition}
    MEMORIA TOTALE (1990) {translated into Italian by
            Beata Della Frattina, as Il Sobborgio Dimenticato}
    WE CAN REMEMBER IT FOR YOU WHOLESALE (1990)
            {Citadel Twilight edition only}

A18. The Cookie Lady (ss)
    Fantasy Fiction 6-53
    A HANDFUL OF DARKNESS (1955)
    MORE MACABRE, Wollheim, Ace, 1961
    EEN HANDVOL DUISTERNIS (1969) {translated into Dutch by
            Henk Bouwman, as Koekjes}
    [televised as J6, 1970s]
    PHILIP K. DICK OMNIBUS (1977) {translated into Dutch by
            Henk Bouwman, as Koekjes}
    ALFRED HITCHCOCK PRESENTS: THE MASTER'S CHOICE,
            Hitchcock, Random House, 1979; Coronet, 1981
            (13 of 27, as AHP: THE MASTER'S CHOICE, BOOK ONE);
    SECOND VARIETY (1987) {not in Citadel Twilight edition}
    HUNGER FOR HORROR, Adams/Adams/Greenberg, DAW, 1988
    WE CAN REMEMBER IT FOR YOU WHOLESALE (1990)
            {Citadel Twilight edition only}

A19. The Cosmic Poachers (ss) ["Burglar"]
      Imagination 7-53
      ALIEN WORLDS, Elwood, Paperback Library, 1964
      EEN SWIBBEL VOOR DAG EN NACHT (1969) {translated into
            Dutch by C.A.G. Von Den Broek, as Kapers in
            Der Cosmos}
      PHILIP K. DICK OMNIBUS (1977) {translated into Dutch by
            C.A.G. Von Den Broek, as Kapers in Der Cosmos}
      SECOND VARIETY (1987) {not in Citadel Twilight edition}
      WE CAN REMEMBER IT FOR YOU WHOLESALE (1990)
            {Citadel Twilight edition only}

A20. The Crawlers (ss) ["Foundling Home"]
      Imagination 7-54
      THE PRESERVING MACHINE AND OTHER STORIES (1969)
      DE ONMOGELIJKE PLANEET (1976) {translated into Dutch
            by Amos Baat, as De Kruipers}
      YOU AND SCIENCE FICTION, Hollister,
            National Textbook Co, 1976
      LES DÉLIRES DIVERGENTS DE PHILIP K. DICK (1979) {translated
            into French by Alain Dorémieux}
      THE FATHER-THING (1987)
      SECOND VARIETY (1991) {Citadel Twilight edition only}

A21. The Crystal Crypt (NT)
      Planet Stories 1-54
      BEYOND LIES THE WUB / THE SHORT HAPPY LIFE OF THE BROWN
            OXFORD (1987)

A22. The Day Mr. Computer Fell out of its Tree (ss)
      THE LITTLE BLACK BOX / THE EYE OF THE SIBYL (1987)
      WE CAN REMEMBER IT FOR YOU WHOLSESALE (1991) {Grafton
            edition only}

A23. The Days of Perky Pat (NT) ["In the Days of Perky Pat"]
      Amazing 12-63
      THE THREE STIGMATA OF PALMER ELDRITCH (1965) {expanded}
      The Most Thrilling SF Ever Told Summer 1968
      EEN SWIBBEL VOOR DAG EN NACHT (1969) {translated into
            Dutch by C.A.G. Von Den Broek, as De Tijd Van
            Hippe Hetty}
      THE BEST OF PHILIP K. DICK (1977)
      PHILIP K. DICK OMNIBUS (1977) {translated into Dutch by
            C.A.G. Von Den Broek, as De Tijd Van Hippe Hetty}
      LE LIVRE D'OR DE LA SCIENCE-FICTION PHILIP K. DICK (1979)
            {translated into French by Marcel Thaon}
      SF ORIGINS, Nolan/Greenberg, Popular Library, 1980
      AMAZING STORIES: 60 YEARS OF THE BEST SCIENCE FICTION,
            Asimov/Greenberg, TSR, 1985
      THE DAYS OF PERKY PAT / THE MINORITY REPORT (1987)

A24. The Defenders (NA)
        Galaxy 1-53; Vol 3 #5, 6-53 (UK);
        [dramatized as J7, 1956]
        THE PENULTIMATE TRUTH (1964) {expanded and adapted}
        INVASION OF THE ROBOTS, Elwood, Paperback Library, 1965
        THE BOOK OF PHILIP K. DICK / THE TURNING WHEEL (1973)
        THERE WILL BE WAR, Pournelle/Carr, Tor, 1983
        Galaktika #52, 1983 {translated into Hungarian, as
                A Védök}
        ROBOTS, ANDROIDS AND MECHANICAL ODDITIES (1984)
        BEYOND LIES THE WUB / THE SHORT HAPPY LIFE OF THE BROWN
                OXFORD (1987)
        BATTLEFIELDS BEYOND TOMORROW, Waugh/Greenberg,
                Crown/Bonanza, 1987

A25. Le Diable (sss)
        The Berkeley Gazette 23-1-42

A26. The Different Stages of Love (ext) {portion of FLOW MY
                TEARS, THE POLICEMAN SAID that was omitted from
                English language editions}
        FLOW MY TEARS, THE POLICEMAN SAID (1975) {French editions
                only} {translated into French}
        PKDS Newsletter (fnz) #28, 3-92

A27. The Electric Ant (NT)
        Fantasy and Science Fiction 10-69
        THE YEAR'S BEST SCIENCE FICTION NO. 3, Harrison/Aldiss,
                Sphere, 1970; Putnam's, 1970 (as BEST SF: 1969);
        DEN ELEKTRISKE MYRE, Storm, Borgen, 1972 {translated into
                Danish, as Den Elektriske Myre}
        WINDOWS INTO TOMORROW, Silverberg, Hawthorn, 1974
        THE BEST OF PHILIP K. DICK (1977)
        DECADE: THE 1960s, Aldiss/Harrison, Macmillan, 1977
        THE ANDROIDS ARE COMING, Silverberg, Elsevier-Nelson, 1979
        SPACE ODYSSEY, Anon, Octopus, 1983
        ROBOTS, ANDROIDS AND MECHANICAL ODDITIES (1984)
        MACHINES THAT THINK, Asimov/Greenberg/Warrick, Holt,
                Rinehart & Winston, 1984
        THE LITTLE BLACK BOX / THE EYE OF THE SIBYL (1987)
        MEMORIA TOTALE (1990) {translated into Italian by
                Angela Campana, as Le Formiche Elettriche}
        WE CAN REMEMBER IT FOR YOU WHOLSESALE (1991) {Grafton
                edition only}

A28. 11-17-80 (ss)
        DIVINE INVASIONS by Lawrence Sutin, Harmony, 1989

A29. Exhibit Piece (ss)
        If 8-54; Vol 1 #13, 11-54 (UK);
        A HANDFUL OF DARKNESS (1955)
        THE FATHER-THING (1987)
        SECOND VARIETY (1991) {Citadel Twilight edition only}

A30. The Exit Door Leads In (NA)
        Rolling Stone College Papers #1, Fall 1979
        THE BEST SCIENCE FICTION OF THE YEAR #9, Carr,
                Ballantine, 1980
        ROBOTS, ANDROIDS AND MECHANICAL ODDITIES (1984)
        I HOPE I SHALL ARRIVE SOON (1985)
        THE LITTLE BLACK BOX / THE EYE OF THE SIBYL (1987)
        WE CAN REMEMBER IT FOR YOU WHOLSESALE (1991) {Grafton
                edition only}

A31. Expendable (ss) ["He Who Waits"]
        Fantasy and Science Fiction 7-53; Vol 1 #4, 1-54 (UK);
                #4, 8-55 (Aust);
        A HANDFUL OF DARKNESS (1955)
        SCIENCE FICTION SHOWCASE, Kornbluth, Doubleday, 1959;
                Curtis, 1969 (11 of 12);
        EEN HANDVOL DUISTERNIS (1969) {translated into Dutch by
                Henk Bouwman, as Slachtoffer}
        THE BEST OF PHILIP K. DICK (1977)
        PHILIP K. DICK OMNIBUS (1977) {translated into Dutch by
                Henk Bouwman, as Slachtoffer}
        BEYOND LIES THE WUB / THE SHORT HAPPY LIFE OF THE BROWN
                OXFORD (1987)
        THE MONSTER BOOK OF MONSTERS, O'Shaughnessy, Xanadu, 1988
        RIVALS OF WEIRD TALES, Weinberg/Dziemianowicz/Greenberg,
                Bonanza, 1990
        MONSTRI DEL CIELO E DELLA TERRA, O'Shaughnessy, Mondadori,
                1991 {translated into Italian by Corinna Augustoni,
                as Sacrificabile}

A32. Explorers We (ss)
        Fantasy and Science Fiction 1-59
        Venture 1-64
        I HOPE I SHALL ARRIVE SOON (1985)
        THE DAYS OF PERKY PAT / THE MINORITY REPORT (1987)

A33. The Eye of the Sibyl (ss)
        PHILIP K. DICK: THE DREAM CONNECTION, Apel,
                Permanent Press, 1987
        THE LITTLE BLACK BOX / THE EYE OF THE SIBYL (1987)
        Gnosis (fnz) #5, 10-87
        WE CAN REMEMBER IT FOR YOU WHOLSESALE (1991) {Grafton
                edition only}

A34. The Eyes Have It (ss)
Science Fiction Stories #1, 1953
101 SCIENCE FICTION STORIES, Greenberg/Waugh/Waugh,
Crown/Avenel, 1986; Magpie, 1992 {as THE GIANT
BOOK OF SCIENCE FICTION STORIES};
THE FATHER-THING (1987)
SECOND VARIETY (1991) {Citadel Twilight edition only}

A35. Fair Game (ss)
If 9-59
THE FATHER-THING (1987)
SECOND VARIETY (1991) {Citadel Twilight edition only}

A36. Faith of Our Fathers (NA)
DANGEROUS VISIONS, Ellison, Doubleday, 1967
ALPHA 2, Silverberg, Ballantine, 1971
MODERN SCIENCE FICTION, Spinrad, Anchor, 1974
THE BEST OF PHILIP K. DICK (1977)
THE LITTLE BLACK BOX / THE EYE OF THE SIBYL (1987)
DANGEROUS VISIONS, Ellison, Mondadori, 1990 {translated
into Italian by Paola Andreaus, as La Fede Dei
Nostri Padri}
WE CAN REMEMBER IT FOR YOU WHOLSESALE (1991) {Grafton
edition only}
FOUNDATIONS OF FEAR, Hartwell, Tor, 1992
Proxima #23 {translated into Danish, as Vore Fædres Tro}

A37. The Father-Thing (ss)
Fantasy and Science Fiction 12-54
A TREASURY OF GREAT SCIENCE FICTION VOL 1, Boucher,
Doubleday, 1959
THE UNHUMANS, Kapp, Popular Library, 1965
TOMORROW'S CHILDREN, Asimov, Doubleday, 1966
THEMES IN SCIENCE FICTION, Kelley, McGraw-Hill, 1972
SCIENCE FICTION 1, Pierce, Houghton Mifflin, 1973
SOCIAL PROBLEMS THROUGH SCIENCE FICTION, Greenberg/
Milstead/Olander/Warrick, St. Martin's, 1975
THE BEST OF PHILIP K. DICK (1977)
SCIENCE FICTION: CONTEMPORARY MYTHOLOGY,
Warrick/Greenberg/Olander, Harper Row, 1978
SCIENCE FICTION: MASTERS OF TODAY, Liebman,
Richards Rosen, 1981
THE GREAT SF STORIES 16 (1954), Asimov/Greenberg, DAW, 1987
THE FATHER-THING (1987)
URBAN HORRORS, Nolan/Greenberg, Dark Harvest, 1990
SECOND VARIETY (1991) {Citadel Twilight edition only}
[staged as J8, 1991]
NURSERY CRIMES, Dziemianowicz/Weinberg/Greenberg,
Barnes & Noble, 1993

A38. Fawn, Look Back (outline for early version of THE OWL IN
          DAYLIGHT)
      Science Fiction Eye (fnz) #2, 8-87

A39. The First Presentation (sss)
      The Berkeley Gazette 22-5-44

A40. Foster, You're Dead! (NA)
      STAR SCIENCE FICTION STORIES NO. 3, Pohl, Ballantine, 1955
      THE BEST OF PHILIP K. DICK (1977)
      THE FATHER-THING (1987)
      SECOND VARIETY (1991) {Citadel Twilight edition only}

  - Frozen Journey {see under I Hope I Shall Arrive Soon}

A41. A Game of Unchance (NT)
      Amazing 7-64
      SF Greats Fall 1970
      LE LIVRE D'OR DE LA SCIENCE-FICTION PHILIP K. DICK (1979)
            {translated into French by Marcel Thaon}
      THE GOLDEN MAN (1980)
      ROBOTS, ANDROIDS AND MECHANICAL ODDITIES (1984)
      THE LITTLE BLACK BOX / THE EYE OF THE SIBYL (1987)
      WE CAN REMEMBER IT FOR YOU WHOLSESALE (1991) {Grafton
            edition only}

A42. A Glass of Darkness (NA)
      Satellite 12-56
      THE COSMIC PUPPETS (1957) {expanded}

A43. The Golden Man (NT) ["The God Who Runs"]
      If 4-54; Vol 1 #9, 7-54 (UK);
      BEYOND THE BARRIERS OF SPACE AND TIME, Merril,
            Random House, 1954
      EVIL EARTHS, Aldiss, Weidenfeld & Nicolson, 1975
      STRANGE GIFTS, Silverberg, Nelson, 1975
      THE GOLDEN MAN (1980)
      DÉDALES DÉMESURÉS DE PHILIP K. DICK (1982) {translated
            into French by Alain Dorémieux & Jean-Pierre Pugi}
      WORLDS OF IF: A RETROSPECTIVE ANTHOLOGY,
            Pohl/Greenberg/Olander, Bluejay, 1986
      THE FATHER-THING (1987)
      SECOND VARIETY (1991) {Citadel Twilight edition only}

A44. Goodbye, Vincent (ss)
      THE DARK-HAIRED GIRL (1988)

A45. The Great C (ss)
Cosmos #1, 9-53
SF Monthly (Aust) #7, 3-56
DEUS IRAE (1976) {expanded and adapted}
BEYOND LIES THE WUB / THE SHORT HAPPY LIFE OF THE BROWN
        OXFORD (1987)

A46. The Gun (ss)
Planet Stories 9-52
SF Monthly (Aust) #12, 8-56
BEYOND LIES THE WUB / THE SHORT HAPPY LIFE OF THE BROWN
        OXFORD (1987)

A47. The Handy Puddle (sss)
The Berkeley Gazette 5-2-42

A48. The Hanging Stranger (ss)
Science Fiction Adventures 12-53
THE FATHER-THING (1987)
SECOND VARIETY (1991) {Citadel Twilight edition only}

A49. The Highbrow (sss)
The Berkeley Gazette 26-10-43

A50. Holy Quarrel (NT)
Worlds of Tomorrow 5-66
I HOPE I SHALL ARRIVE SOON (1985)
THE LITTLE BLACK BOX / THE EYE OF THE SIBYL (1987)
MEMORIA TOTALE (1990) {translated into Italian by
        Vittorio Curtoni, as Teologia per Computer}
WE CAN REMEMBER IT FOR YOU WHOLSESALE (1991) {Grafton
        edition only}

A51. The Hood Maker (ss) ["Immunity"]
Imagination 6-55
SECOND VARIETY (1987) {not in Citadel Twilight edition}
WE CAN REMEMBER IT FOR YOU WHOLESALE (1990)
        {Citadel Twilight edition only}

A52. Human Is (ss)
Startling Stories Winter 1955
THE BEST OF PHILIP K. DICK (1977)
LE LIVRE D'OR DE LA SCIENCE-FICTION PHILIP K. DICK (1979)
        {translated into French by Marcel Thaon}
SECOND VARIETY (1987) {not in Citadel Twilight edition}
WE CAN REMEMBER IT FOR YOU WHOLESALE (1990)
        {Citadel Twilight edition only}
[staged as J12, 1991]

A53. If There Were No Benny Cemoli (ss) ["Had There Never Been
        a Benny Cemoli"]
    Galaxy 12-63
    THE EIGHTH GALAXY READER, Pohl, Doubleday, 1965;
        Curtis, 1965 (as FINAL ENCOUNTER)
    THE PRESERVING MACHINE AND OTHER STORIES (1969)
    THE BEST OF PHILIP K. DICK (1977)
    MACHINES THAT THINK, Asimov/Greenberg/Warrick, Holt,
        Rinehart & Winston, 1984
    THE DAYS OF PERKY PAT / THE MINORITY REPORT (1987)
    THE GREAT SF STORIES 25 (1963), Asimov/Greenberg, DAW, 1992

A54. I Hope I Shall Arrive Soon (ss)
    Playboy 12-80 {as Frozen Journey}
    THE BEST SCIENCE FICTION OF THE YEAR #10, Carr,
        Pocket, 1981 {as Frozen Journey}
    ROBOTS, ANDROIDS AND MECHANICAL ODDITIES (1984)
        {as Frozen Journey}
    FASEKIFT, Holm, Dansklærerforengingen, 1984
        {translated into Danish, as Fastfrosset I Rejsen}
    I HOPE I SHALL ARRIVE SOON (1985)
    THE LITTLE BLACK BOX / THE EYE OF THE SIBYL (1987)
    WE CAN REMEMBER IT FOR YOU WHOLSESALE (1991) {Grafton
        edition only}
    Portti 7-93 {translated into Finnish}
    SIMULATIONS, Jacobson, Citadel Twilight, 1993
    THE NORTON BOOK OF SCIENCE FICTION, Le Guin/Attebery,
        Norton, 1993 {as Frozen Journey}

  - I Killed the Bumble Bee {see under Once There Was
        An Ant}

A55. The Impossible Planet (ss) ["Legend"]
    Imagination 10-53
    A HANDFUL OF DARKNESS (1955)
    EEN HANDVOL DUISTERNIS (1969) {translated into Dutch by
        Henk Bouwman, as De Onmogelijke Planeet}
    SPACE ODYSSEYS, Aldiss, Orbit, 1974
    DE ONMOGELIJKE PLANEET (1976) {translated into Dutch
        by Henk Bouwman, as De Onmogelijke Planeet}
    LE LIVRE D'OR DE LA SCIENCE-FICTION PHILIP K. DICK (1979)
        {translated into French by Marcel Thaon, as La
        Planete Impossibile}
    L'ANNÉÉ 1978-1979 DE LA SCIENCE-FICTION ET DU FANTASTIQUE,
        Goimard, Juillard, 1979 {translated into French by
        Marcel Thaon, as La Planete Impossibile}
    SCIENCE FICTION, Raun, Forlaget Systime, 1983 {translated
        into Danish, as Den Umulige Planet}
    SECOND VARIETY (1987) {not in Citadel Twilight edition}
    WE CAN REMEMBER IT FOR YOU WHOLESALE (1990)
        {Citadel Twilight edition only}

A56. Impostor (ss)
       Astounding 6-53; 11-53 (UK)
       A HANDFUL OF DARKNESS (1955)
       SCIENCE FICTION TERROR TALES, Conklin, Gnome, 1955
       BEST SF 2, Crispin, Faber, 1956
       THE END OF THE WORLD, Wollheim, Ace, 1956
       [televised as J13, 1962]
       UNTRAVELLED WORLDS, Barter/Wilson, Macmillan, 1966
       THE METAL SMILE, Knight, Belmont, 1968
       EEN HANDVOL DUISTERNIS (1969) {translated into Dutch by
              Henk Bouwman, as De Bedrieger}
       DARK STARS, Silverberg, Ballantine, 1969
       THE ASTOUNDING-ANALOG READER: VOLUME TWO, Harrison/Aldiss,
              Doubleday, 1973
       DE ONMOGELIJKE PLANEET (1976) {translated into Dutch
              by Henk Bouwman, as De Bedrieger}
       THE BEST OF PHILIP K. DICK (1977)
       SOULS IN METAL, Ashley, Hale, 1977
       THE ARBOR HOUSE TREASURY OF MODERN SCIENCE FICTION,
              Silverberg/Greenberg, Arbor House, 1980;
              Crown/Avenel, 1987 (37 of 38) (as GREAT
              SCIENCE FICTION OF THE 20TH CENTURY)
       WIDE-ANGLE LENS, Fenner, Morrow, 1980
       ROBOTS, ANDROIDS AND MECHANICAL ODDITIES (1984)
       PHILOSOPHY AND SCIENCE FICTION, Phillips, Prometheus, 1984
       THE GREAT SF STORIES 15 (1953), Asimov/Greenberg, DAW, 1986
       SECOND VARIETY (1987) {not in Citadel Twilight edition}
       [broadcast as J14, 1989]
       WE CAN REMEMBER IT FOR YOU WHOLESALE (1990)
              {Citadel Twilight edition only}
       INVASIONS, Asimov/Greenberg/Waugh, Roc, 1990
       RACCONTI BREVI II, Drago, Milano, 1990 {translated into
              Italian by Ferruccio Alessandri, as L'Impostore}
       LE MERAVIGLIE DEL POSSIBILE, Solmi/Fruttero, Einaudi, 1991
              {translated into Italian by Floriana Bossi, as
              Impostore}

A57. The Indefatigable Frog (ss)
       Fantastic Story Magazine 7-53
       A HANDFUL OF DARKNESS (1955)
       Alt For Mænd 7-69 {translated into Danish, as Den
              Utrættelige Frø}
       LES DÉLIRES DIVERGENTS DE PHILIP K. DICK (1979) {translated
              into French by Alain Dorémieux}
       BEYOND LIES THE WUB / THE SHORT HAPPY LIFE OF THE BROWN
              OXFORD (1987)
       THE ASCENT OF WONDER, Hartwell/Cramer, Tor, 1994

A58. The Infinites (ss)
       Planet Stories 5-53
       SF Monthly (Aust) #18, 2-57
       BEYOND LIES THE WUB / THE SHORT HAPPY LIFE OF THE BROWN
              OXFORD (1987)

A59. James P. Crow (ss)
   Planet Stories 5-54
   SECOND VARIETY (1987) {not in Citadel Twilight edition}
   WE CAN REMEMBER IT FOR YOU WHOLESALE (1990)
        {Citadel Twilight edition only}

A60. Joe Protagoras is Alive and Living on Earth (outline)
   NEW WORLDS 2, Garnett, Gollancz, 1992

A61. Jon's World (NT) ["Jon"]
   TIME TO COME, Derleth, Farrar, 1954; Berkley, 1958
        (10 of 12); Tower, 1965 (10 of 12);
   SECOND VARIETY (1987) {not in Citadel Twilight edition}
   WE CAN REMEMBER IT FOR YOU WHOLESALE (1990)
        {Citadel Twilight edition only}

A62. Jungle People (sss)
   The Berkeley Gazette 17-2-42

A63. The King of the Elves (ss) ["Shadrach Jones and the Elves"]
   Beyond 9-53
   THE GOLDEN MAN (1980)
   BEYOND LIES THE WUB / THE SHORT HAPPY LIFE OF THE BROWN
        OXFORD (1987)
   MASTERPIECES OF FANTASY AND ENCHANTMENT, Hartwell,
        SFBC, 1988
   FAERIES, Asimov/Greenberg/Waugh, Roc, 1991
   SPELLS OF ENCHANTMENT, Zipes, Viking, 1991
   THE OXFORD BOOK OF MODERN FAIRY TALES, Lurie,
        Oxford University Press, 1993

A64. Knight Fight! (sss)
   The Berkeley Gazette 27-10-42

A65. The Last of the Masters (NT) ["Protection Agency"]
   Orbit SF #5, 11/12-54
   SPACE STATION 42 AND OTHER STORIES, Anon, Jubilee, 1958
   THE GOLDEN MAN (1980)
   ROBOTS, ANDROIDS AND MECHANICAL ODDITIES (1984)
   THE FATHER-THING (1987)
   SECOND VARIETY (1991) {Citadel Twilight edition only}

A66. The Little Black Box (NT) ["From Ordinary Household Objects"]
        Worlds of Tomorrow 8-64
        DO ANDROIDS DREAM OF ELECTRIC SHEEP? (1968) {expanded &
                adapted}
        THE GOLDEN MAN (1980)
        DÉDALES DÉMESURÉS DE PHILIP K. DICK (1982) {translated
                into French by Alain Dorémieux & Jean-Pierre Pugi}
        THE LITTLE BLACK BOX / THE EYE OF THE SIBYL (1987)
        WE CAN REMEMBER IT FOR YOU WHOLSESALE (1991) {Grafton
                edition only}

A67. The Little Movement (ss)
        Fantasy and Science Fiction 11-52
        A HANDFUL OF DARKNESS (1955) {not in Panther or Grafton
                editions}
        THE EUREKA YEARS, McComas, Bantam, 1982
        ROBOTS, ANDROIDS AND MECHANICAL ODDITIES (1984)
        BEYOND LIES THE WUB / THE SHORT HAPPY LIFE OF THE BROWN
                OXFORD (1987)
        MEMORIA TOTALE (1990) {translated into Italian by
                Beata Della Frattina, as Minibattaglia}

A68. A Little Something for Us Tempunauts (ss)
        FINAL STAGE, Ferman/Malzberg, Penguin, 1975 (abridged
                version published by Charterhouse, 1974)
        THE BEST SCIENCE FICTION OF THE YEAR #4, Carr,
                Ballantine, 1975
        THE BEST OF PHILIP K. DICK (1977)
        THE LITTLE BLACK BOX / THE EYE OF THE SIBYL (1987)
        THE DARK DESCENT, Hartwell, Tor, 1987; Grafton, 1991
                (17 of 56, as THE DARK DESCENT: A FABULOUS
                FORMLESS DARKNESS);
        WE CAN REMEMBER IT FOR YOU WHOLSESALE (1991) {Grafton
                edition only}

A69. The Magician's Box (sss)
        The Berkeley Gazette 7-2-44

A70. Martians Come in Clouds (ss) ["The Buggies"]
        Fantastic Universe 6/7-53
        SECOND VARIETY (1987) {not in Citadel Twilight edition}
        WE CAN REMEMBER IT FOR YOU WHOLESALE (1990)
                {Citadel Twilight edition only}

A71. Meddler (ss)
        Future 10-54
        THE GOLDEN MAN (1980)
        BEYOND LIES THE WUB / THE SHORT HAPPY LIFE OF THE BROWN
                OXFORD (1987)

A72. The Minority Report (NT)
      Fantastic Universe 1-56
      THE VARIABLE MAN AND OTHER STORIES (1957)
      EEN SWIBBEL VOOR DAG EN NACHT (1969) {translated into
              Dutch by C.A.G. Von Den Broek, as Het Minderheids
              Rapport}
      PHILIP K. DICK OMNIBUS (1977) {translated into Dutch by
              C.A.G. Von Den Broek, as Het Minderheids Rapport}
      THE DAYS OF PERKY PAT / THE MINORITY REPORT (1987)
      MEMORIA TOTALE (1990) {translated into Italian by
              Beata Della Frattina, as Rapporto di Minoranza}

A73. Misadjustment (ss)
      Science Fiction Quarterly 2-57
      LE LIVRE D'OR DE LA SCIENCE-FICTION PHILIP K. DICK (1979)
              {translated into French by Marcel Thaon}
      THE FATHER-THING (1987)
      SECOND VARIETY (1991) {Citadel Twilight edition only}

A74. The Mold of Yancy (NT)
      If 8-55
      THE SECOND WORLD OF IF, Quinn/Wulff, Quinn, 1958
      THE PENULTIMATE TRUTH (1964) {expanded and adapted}
      THE GOLDEN MAN (1980)
      THE DAYS OF PERKY PAT / THE MINORITY REPORT (1987)

A75. Mr. Spaceship (NT)
      Imagination 1-53
      BEYOND LIES THE WUB / THE SHORT HAPPY LIFE OF THE BROWN
              OXFORD (1987)

A76. The Name of the Game is Death (outline for a science fiction
              novel, later extensively reworked as A MAZE OF DEATH)
      NEW WORLDS 2, Garnett, Gollancz, 1992

A77. Nanny (ss)
      Startling Stories Spring 1955
      THE BOOK OF PHILIP K. DICK / THE TURNING WHEEL (1973)
      Galaktika #52, 1983 {translated into Hungarian, as Dadus}
      BEYOND LIES THE WUB / THE SHORT HAPPY LIFE OF THE BROWN
              OXFORD (1987)

A78. Not By Its Cover (ss)
    Famous SF Summer 1968
    THE GOLDEN MAN (1980)
    DÉDALES DÉMESURÉS DE PHILIP K. DICK (1982) {translated
        into French by Alain Dorémieux & Jean-Pierre Pugi}
    THE LITTLE BLACK BOX / THE EYE OF THE SIBYL (1987)
    WE CAN REMEMBER IT FOR YOU WHOLSESALE (1991) {Grafton
        edition only}

A79. Novelty Act (NT) ["At Second Jug"]
    Fantastic 2-64
    THE SIMULACRA (1964) {expanded and adapted}
    THE HUMAN EQUATION, Nolan, Sherbourne, 1971
    THE DAYS OF PERKY PAT / THE MINORITY REPORT (1987)
    FANTASTIC STORIES: TALES OF THE WEIRD AND WONDROUS,
        Greenberg/Price, TSR, 1987

A80. Null-O (ss) ["Loony Lemuel"]
    If 12-58
    THE FATHER-THING (1987)
    SECOND VARIETY (1991) {Citadel Twilight edition only}

A81. Of Withered Apples (ss)
    Cosmos #4, 7-54
    SECOND VARIETY (1987) {not in Citadel Twilight edition}
    WE CAN REMEMBER IT FOR YOU WHOLESALE (1990)
        {Citadel Twilight edition only}

A82. Oh, To Be A Blobel! (ss) ["Well, See, There Were These
        Blobels"]
    Galaxy 2-64
    WORLD'S BEST SCIENCE FICTION: 1965, Wollheim/Carr,
        Ace, 1965
    THE PRESERVING MACHINE AND OTHER STORIES (1969)
    INFINITE JESTS, Silverberg, Chilton, 1974
    THE BEST OF PHILIP K. DICK (1977)
    ALIENS!, Dozois/Dann, Pocket, 1980
    GALAXY: THIRTY YEARS OF INNOVATIVE SCIENCE FICTION,
        Pohl/Olander/Greenberg, Playboy, 1980
    YESTERDAY'S TOMORROWS, Pohl, Berkley, 1982
    THE DAYS OF PERKY PAT / THE MINORITY REPORT (1987)
    Portti 7-93 {translated into Finnish}

A83. Once There Was an Ant (sss)
    PKDS Newsletter (fnz) #3, 4-84 {as I Killed the
        Bumble Bee}
    TO THE HIGH CASTLE by Gregg Rickman, Fragments West, 1989

A84. Orpheus with Clay Feet (ss)
    Escapade -64 {as by Jack Dowland}
    THE DAYS OF PERKY PAT / THE MINORITY REPORT (1987)

A85. Our Friends from Frolix 8 (N)
    OUR FRIENDS FROM FROLIX 8 (1970)
    PKDS Newsletter (fnz) #19, 1-89 {outline}

A86. Out in the Garden (ss)
    Fantasy Fiction 8-53
    SATAN'S PETS, Ghidalia, Manor, 1972
    BEYOND LIES THE WUB / THE SHORT HAPPY LIFE OF THE BROWN
        OXFORD (1987)

A87. Paycheck (NT)
    Imagination 6-53
    THE BEST OF PHILIP K. DICK (1977)
    BEYOND LIES THE WUB / THE SHORT HAPPY LIFE OF THE BROWN
        OXFORD (1987)

A88. Pay for the Printer (ss) ["Printer's Pay"]
    Satellite 10-56
    THE PRESERVING MACHINE AND OTHER STORIES (1969)
    DE ONMOGELIJKE PLANEET (1976) {translated into Dutch
        by Amos Baat, as De Dood Van De Biltongs}
    LE LIVRE D'OR DE LA SCIENCE-FICTION PHILIP K. DICK (1979)
        {translated into French by Marcel Thaon}
    THE FATHER-THING (1987)
    SECOND VARIETY (1991) {Citadel Twilight edition only}

A89. Piper in the Woods (ss)
    Imagination 2-53
    Popular Science Fiction (Aust) Vol 1 #2, 11-53
    OTHER WORLDS, OTHER TIMES, Moskowitz/Elwood, McFadden, 1969
    BEYOND LIES THE WUB / THE SHORT HAPPY LIFE OF THE BROWN
        OXFORD (1987)

A90. The Pirate (sss)
    The Berkeley Gazette 7-10-42

A91. Planet for Transients (ss) ["The Itinerants"]
Fantastic Universe 10/11-53
A HANDFUL OF DARKNESS (1955)
EEN HANDVOL DUISTERNIS (1969) {translated into Dutch by
Henk Bouwman, as Passanten}
DEUS IRAE (1976) {expanded and adapted}
PHILIP K. DICK OMNIBUS (1977) {translated into Dutch by
Henk Bouwman, as Passanten}
SECOND VARIETY (1987) {not in Citadel Twilight edition}
WE CAN REMEMBER IT FOR YOU WHOLESALE (1990)
{Citadel Twilight edition only}

A92. Precious Artifact (ss)
Galaxy 10-64
LES DÉLIRES DIVERGENTS DE PHILIP K. DICK (1979) {translated
into French by Alain Dorémieux}
THE GOLDEN MAN (1980)
THE LITTLE BLACK BOX / THE EYE OF THE SIBYL (1987)
MEMORIA TOTALE (1990) {translated into Italian by
Giovanni Boselli, as Il Gatto}
WE CAN REMEMBER IT FOR YOU WHOLSESALE (1991) {Grafton
edition only}

A93. The Pre-Persons (NA)
Fantasy and Science Fiction 10-74
LES DÉLIRES DIVERGENTS DE PHILIP K. DICK (1979) {translated
into French by Alain Dorémieux}
THE GOLDEN MAN (1980)
THE LITTLE BLACK BOX / THE EYE OF THE SIBYL (1987)
WE CAN REMEMBER IT FOR YOU WHOLSESALE (1991) {Grafton
edition only}

A94. A Present for Pat (ss)
Startling Stories 1-54; #17, 3-54 (UK);
Science Fiction Yearbook #4, 1970
THE BOOK OF PHILIP K. DICK / THE TURNING WHEEL (1973)
Galaktika #52, 1983 {translated into Hungarian, as
Pat Ajándéka}
SECOND VARIETY (1987) {not in Citadel Twilight edition}
WE CAN REMEMBER IT FOR YOU WHOLESALE (1990)
{Citadel Twilight edition only}

A95. The Preserving Machine (ss)
Fantasy and Science Fiction 6-53
A HANDFUL OF DARKNESS (1955) {not in Panther or Grafton
editions}
THE PRESERVING MACHINE AND OTHER STORIES (1969)
THE SCIENCE FICTION BESTIARY, Silverberg, Nelson, 1971
ROBOTS, ANDROIDS AND MECHANICAL ODDITIES (1984)
BEYOND LIES THE WUB / THE SHORT HAPPY LIFE OF THE BROWN
OXFORD (1987)

A96. Prize Ship (NT) ["Globe from Ganymede"]
    Thrilling Wonder Stories Winter 1954
    Enigmas #15, 4-57 {translated into Spanish, as Billete de
        Ida y de Vuelta en el Tiempo}
    BEYOND LIES THE WUB / THE SHORT HAPPY LIFE OF THE BROWN
        OXFORD (1987)

A97. Progeny (ss)
    If 11-54
    A HANDFUL OF DARKNESS (1955)
    EEN HANDVOL DUISTERNIS (1969) {translated into Dutch by
        Henk Bouwman, as Kroost}
    SCHOOL & SOCIETY THROUGH SCIENCE FICTION,
        Olander/Greenberg, Random House, 1974
    MARRIAGE AND THE FAMILY THROUGH SCIENCE FICTION, Clear/
        Warrick/Greenberg/Olander, St. Martin's, 1976
    PHILIP K. DICK OMNIBUS (1977) {translated into Dutch by
        Henk Bouwman, as Kroost}
    SECOND VARIETY (1987) {not in Citadel Twilight edition}
    WE CAN REMEMBER IT FOR YOU WHOLESALE (1990)
        {Citadel Twilight edition only}

A98. Project: Earth (NT) ["One Who Stole"]
    Imagination 12-53
    SECOND VARIETY (1987) {not in Citadel Twilight edition}
    WE CAN REMEMBER IT FOR YOU WHOLESALE (1990)
        {Citadel Twilight edition only}

A99. Project Plowshare (N-2)
    Worlds of Tomorrow 11-65, 1-66
    THE ZAP GUN (1967)

A100. Prominent Author (ss)
    If 5-54; #10, 8-54 (UK);
    A HANDFUL OF DARKNESS (1955)
    SECOND VARIETY (1987) {not in Citadel Twilight edition}
    WE CAN REMEMBER IT FOR YOU WHOLESALE (1990)
        {Citadel Twilight edition only}

A101. Psi-Man Heal My Child! (NT) ["Outside Consultant"]
    Imaginative Tales 11-55
    THE BOOK OF PHILIP K. DICK / THE TURNING WHEEL (1973)
        {as Psi-Man}
    Galaktika #52, 1983 {translated into Hungarian, as A Pszi}
    THE FATHER-THING (1987)
    SECOND VARIETY (1991) {Citadel Twilight edition only}

A102. Puttering About in a Small Land (N)
        The Missouri Review Vol VII #2, 1984 {extract}
        PUTTERING ABOUT IN A SMALL LAND (1985)

A103. Rautavaara's Case (ss)
        Omni 10-80
        NEBULA AWARD STORIES 16, Pournelle/Carr,
            Holt, Rinehart & Winston, 1982
        THE BEST OF OMNI SCIENCE FICTION NO. 5, Bova/Myrus,
            Omni, 1983
        I HOPE I SHALL ARRIVE SOON (1985)
        THE THIRD OMNI BOOK OF SCIENCE FICTION, Datlow, Zebra, 1985
        THE LITTLE BLACK BOX / THE EYE OF THE SIBYL (1987)
        WE CAN REMEMBER IT FOR YOU WHOLSESALE (1991) {Grafton
            edition only}
        Portti 7-93 {translated into Finnish}

A104. Recall Mechanism (ss)
        [dramatized as J16, 1958]
        If 7-59
        LE LIVRE D'OR DE LA SCIENCE-FICTION PHILIP K. DICK (1979)
            {translated into French by Marcel Thaon}
        THE DAYS OF PERKY PAT / THE MINORITY REPORT (1987)

  -   Retreat from Rigel {see under Tony and the Beetles}

A105. Retreat Syndrome (NT)
        Worlds of Tomorrow 1-65
        THE PRESERVING MACHINE AND OTHER STORIES (1969)
        LES DÉLIRES DIVERGENTS DE PHILIP K. DICK (1979) {translated
            into French by Alain Dorémieux}
        THE LITTLE BLACK BOX / THE EYE OF THE SIBYL (1987)
        WE CAN REMEMBER IT FOR YOU WHOLSESALE (1991) {Grafton
            edition only}

A106. Return Match (ss)
        Galaxy 2-67; 9/10-67 (UK);
        LES DÉLIRES DIVERGENTS DE PHILIP K. DICK (1979) {translated
            into French by Alain Dorémieux}
        THE GOLDEN MAN (1980)
        Starlog #51, 10-81
        THE LITTLE BLACK BOX / THE EYE OF THE SIBYL (1987)
        WE CAN REMEMBER IT FOR YOU WHOLSESALE (1991) {Grafton
            edition only}

A107. Roog (ss) ["Friday Morning"]
     Fantasy and Science Fiction 2-53
     THE PRESERVING MACHINE AND OTHER STORIES (1969)
     THE OTHERS, Carr, Fawcett, 1969
     INVADERS FROM SPACE, Silverberg, Hawthorn, 1972
     REFLECTIONS OF THE FUTURE, Hill, Ginn, 1975
     DE ONMOGELIJKE PLANEET (1976) {translated into Dutch
         by Amos Baat, as Groem}
     THE BEST OF PHILIP K. DICK (1977)
     Unearth Winter 1979
     LES DÉLIRES DIVERGENTS DE PHILIP K. DICK (1979) {translated
         into French by Alain Dorémieux}
     BEYOND LIES THE WUB / THE SHORT HAPPY LIFE OF THE BROWN
         OXFORD (1987)
     DOGTALES, Dann/Dozois, Ace, 1988
     INVADERS!, Dann/Dozois, Ace, 1993

A108. Sales Pitch (NT)
     Future 6-54
     THE GOLDEN MAN (1980)
     ROBOTS, ANDROIDS AND MECHANICAL ODDITIES (1984)
     THE FATHER-THING (1987)
     [broadcast as J25, 1989]
     SECOND VARIETY (1991) {Citadel Twilight edition only}

A109. Santa's Return (sss)
     The Berkeley Gazette 4-1-44
     TO THE HIGH CASTLE by Gregg Rickman, Fragments West, 1989

A110. Second Variety (NT)
     Space SF 5-53
     YEAR'S BEST SCIENCE FICTION NOVELS 1954, Bleiler/Dikty,
         Fell, 1954; Grayson, 1955 (as THE YEAR'S BEST
         SCIENCE FICTION NOVELS: SECOND SERIES);
     Selected Science-Fiction (Aust) #1, 5-55
     THE VARIABLE MAN AND OTHER STORIES (1957)
     SPECTRUM II, Amis/Conquest, Gollancz, 1962
     EEN HANDVOL DUISTERNIS (1969) {translated into Dutch by
         Henk Bouwman, as Type Twee}
     THE BEST OF PHILIP K. DICK (1977)
     PHILIP K. DICK OMNIBUS (1977) {translated into Dutch by
         Henk Bouwman, as Type Twee}
     BEST SCIENCE FICTION STORIES, Stapleton, Hamlyn, 1977
     ANDEN UNGAVE (1982)
     ROBOTS, ANDROIDS AND MECHANICAL ODDITIES (1984)
     MACHINES THAT KILL, Saberhagen/Greenberg, Ace, 1984
     SECOND VARIETY (1987)
     ROBOTS, Asimov/Greenberg/Waugh, Signet, 1989
     THE WORLD TREASURY OF SCIENCE FICTION, Hartwell,
         Little, Brown, 1989
     [dramatized as J3]

A110. Second Variety (cont)
MEMORIA TOTALE (1990) {translated into Italian by
Beata Della Frattina, as Modello Due}
ROBOT WARRIORS, Waugh/Greenberg, Ace, 1991
Nowa Fantastyka #5, 1992 {translated into Polish}

A111. Service Call (ss)
SF Stories 7-55
MASTERS OF SCIENCE FICTION, (Howard), Belmont, 1964
EEN SWIBBEL VOOR DAG EN NACHT (1969) {translated into
Dutch by C.A.G. Von Den Broek, as Een Swibbel
Voor dag en Nacht}
THE BEST OF PHILIP K. DICK (1977)
PHILIP K. DICK OMNIBUS (1977) {translated into Dutch by
C.A.G. Von Den Broek, as Een Swibbel Voor dag
en Nacht}
DÉDALES DÉMESURÉS DE PHILIP K. DICK (1982) {translated
into French by Alain Dorémieux & Jean-Pierre Pugi}
ROBOTS, ANDROIDS AND MECHANICAL ODDITIES (1984)
THE DAYS OF PERKY PAT / THE MINORITY REPORT (1987)

A112. Shell Game (ss)
Galaxy 9-54
CLANS OF THE ALPHANE MOON (1964) {expanded and adapted}
THE BOOK OF PHILIP K. DICK / THE TURNING WHEEL (1973)
LE LIVRE D'OR DE LA SCIENCE-FICTION PHILIP K. DICK (1979)
{translated into French by Marcel Thaon}
Galaktika #52, 1983 {translated into Hungarian, as Háborúsdi}
THE FATHER-THING (1987)
SECOND VARIETY (1991) {Citadel Twilight edition only}

A113. The Short Happy Life of the Brown Oxford (ss) ["Left Shoe,
My Foot"]
Fantasy and Science Fiction 1-54; Vol 3 #1, 6-54 (UK);
I HOPE I SHALL ARRIVE SOON (1985)
BEYOND LIES THE WUB / THE SHORT HAPPY LIFE OF THE BROWN
OXFORD (1987)
[broadcast as J26, 1993]

A114. The Skull (NT)
If 9-52
BEYOND LIES THE WUB / THE SHORT HAPPY LIFE OF THE BROWN
OXFORD (1987)

A115. The Slave Race (sss)
The Berkeley Gazette 8-5-44
TO THE HIGH CASTLE by Gregg Rickman, Fragments West, 1989

A116. Small Town (ss) ["Engineer"]
    Amazing 5-54; Vol 1 #5, 8-54 (UK);
    Amazing 4-67
    EEN SWIBBEL VOOR DAG EN NACHT (1969) {translated into
        Dutch by C.A.G. Von Den Broek, as Kleinsteeds}
    PHILIP K. DICK OMNIBUS (1977) {translated into Dutch by
        C.A.G. Von Den Broek, as Kleinsteeds}
    Fiction #294, 10-78 {translated into French, as Petite Ville}
    LE LIVRE D'OR DE LA SCIENCE-FICTION PHILIP K. DICK (1979)
        {translated into French by Marcel Thaon, as
        Petite Ville}
    THE GOLDEN MAN (1980)
    SECOND VARIETY (1987) {not in Citadel Twilight edition}
    WE CAN REMEMBER IT FOR YOU WHOLESALE (1990)
        {Citadel Twilight edition only}

A117. Some Kinds of Life (ss) ["The Beleagured"]
    Fantastic Universe 10/11-53 {as by Richard Phillips}
    SECOND VARIETY (1987) {not in Citadel Twilight edition}
    WE CAN REMEMBER IT FOR YOU WHOLESALE (1990)
        {Citadel Twilight edition only}

A118. Souvenir (ss)
    Fantastic Universe 10-54
    SECOND VARIETY (1987) {not in Citadel Twilight edition}
    WE CAN REMEMBER IT FOR YOU WHOLESALE (1990)
        {Citadel Twilight edition only}

A119. Stability (ss)
    BEYOND LIES THE WUB / THE SHORT HAPPY LIFE OF THE BROWN
        OXFORD (1987)

A120. Stand-By (ss)
    Amazing 10-63
    THE CRACK IN SPACE (1966) {expanded and adapted}
    THE PRESERVING MACHINE AND OTHER STORIES (1969)
        {as Top Stand-By Job}
    INSIDE INFORMATION, Mowshowitz, Addison-Wesley, 1977
        {as Top Stand-By Job}
    LE LIVRE D'OR DE LA SCIENCE-FICTION PHILIP K. DICK (1979)
        {translated into French by Marcel Thaon}
    WHAT IF? VOLUME 2, Lupoff, Pocket, 1981
    THE DAYS OF PERKY PAT / THE MINORITY REPORT (1987)

A121. The Story to End All Stories for Harlan Ellison's Anthology
        DANGEROUS VISIONS (sss)
      Niekas (fnz) #20, Fall 1968
      THE LITTLE BLACK BOX / THE EYE OF THE SIBYL (1987)
      WE CAN REMEMBER IT FOR YOU WHOLSESALE (1991) {Grafton
        edition only}
      Forum Fabulatorum (fnz) #10 {translated into Danish, as
        Den Sidste Historie}

A122. Strange Eden (ss) ["Immolation"]
      Imagination 12-54
      THE FATHER-THING (1987)
      SECOND VARIETY (1991) {Citadel Twilight edition only}

A123. Strange Memories of Death (ss)
      Interzone #8, Summer 1984
      I HOPE I SHALL ARRIVE SOON (1985)
      THE LITTLE BLACK BOX / THE EYE OF THE SIBYL (1987)
      WE CAN REMEMBER IT FOR YOU WHOLSESALE (1991) {Grafton
        edition only}

A124. Stratosphere Betsy (1st part of series)
      The Truth (self-published newspaper) 30-8-43

A125. A Surface Raid (NT)
      Fantastic Universe 7-55
      SECOND VARIETY (1987) {not in Citadel Twilight edition}
      WE CAN REMEMBER IT FOR YOU WHOLESALE (1990)
        {Citadel Twilight edition only}

A126. Survey Team (ss)
      Fantastic Universe 5-54
      SECOND VARIETY (1987) {not in Citadel Twilight edition}
      WE CAN REMEMBER IT FOR YOU WHOLESALE (1990)
        {Citadel Twilight edition only}

A127. A Terran Odyssey (NA) (put together by Dick from sections of
        DR. BLOODMONEY)
      THE LITTLE BLACK BOX / THE EYE OF THE SIBYL (1987)
      WE CAN REMEMBER IT FOR YOU WHOLSESALE (1991) {Grafton
        edition only}

A128. Time Out of Joint (N-3)
      TIME OUT OF JOINT (1959)
      New Worlds #89, 90, 91, 12-59, 1, 2-60 (abridged)

A129. Time Pawn (SN)
        Thrilling Wonder Stories Summer 1954
        DR. FUTURITY (1960) {expanded}

A130. Today the World (unfinished story)
        PKDS Newsletter (fnz) #20, 4-89

A131. Tony and the Beetles (ss)
        Orbit SF #2, 1954
        PLANET OF DOOM AND OTHER STORIES, Anon, Jubilee, 1958
            {as Retreat from Rigel}
        THE FATHER-THING (1987)
        SECOND VARIETY (1991) {Citadel Twilight edition only}

  -   Top Stand-By Job {see under Stand-By}

A132. To Serve the Master (ss) ["Be As Gods"]
        Imagination 2-56
        ROBOTS, ANDROIDS AND MECHANICAL ODDITIES (1984)
        THE FATHER-THING (1987)
        SECOND VARIETY (1991) {Citadel Twilight edition only}

A133. The Trouble with Bubbles (ss) ["Plaything"]
        If 9-53; Vol 1 #4, 2-54 (UK);
        SECOND VARIETY (1987) {not in Citadel Twilight edition}
        WE CAN REMEMBER IT FOR YOU WHOLESALE (1990)
            {Citadel Twilight edition only}

A134. The Turning Wheel (ss)
        SF Stories #2, 1954
        A HANDFUL OF DARKNESS (1955)
        NOW & BEYOND, Howard, Belmont, 1965
        THE BOOK OF PHILIP K. DICK / THE TURNING WHEEL (1973)
        Galaktika #52, 1983 {translated into Hungarian, as
            A Sors Kereke}
        THE FATHER-THING (1987)
        IMPERIAL STARS, VOL. 2: REPUBLIC AND EMPIRE, Pournelle,
            Baen, 1987
        SECOND VARIETY (1991) {Citadel Twilight edition only}

A135. The Unreconstructed M (NT)
        SF Stories 1-57
        THE GOLDEN MAN (1980)
        THE DAYS OF PERKY PAT / THE MINORITY REPORT (1987)

A136. The Unteleported Man (SN)
         Fantastic 12-64
         THE UNTELEPORTED MAN / LIES INC. (1966)
         PKDS Newsletter (fnz) #8, 9-85 {the missing pages}

A137. Upon the Dull Earth (NT)
         Beyond Fantasy Fiction #9, 1954
         A HANDFUL OF DARKNESS (1955)
         THE PRESERVING MACHINE AND OTHER STORIES (1969)
         EEN HANDVOL DUISTERNIS (1969) {translated into Dutch by
             Henk Bouwman, as De Saaie Aarde}
         THE 2ND MAYFLOWER BOOK OF BLACK MAGIC STORIES, Parry,
             Mayflower, 1974
         PHILIP K. DICK OMNIBUS (1977) {translated into Dutch by
             Henk Bouwman, as De Saaie Aarde}
         THE FATHER-THING (1987)
         FINE FRIGHTS, Campbell, Tor, 1988
         SECOND VARIETY (1991) {Citadel Twilight edition only}
         PAURE ECCELLENTI, Campbell, Mondadori, 1991 {translated
             into Italian by Massimo Patti, as Sopra Questo
             Cupo Mondo}

A138. The Variable Man (NA)
         Space SF 9-53; 7-53 (UK);
         THE VARIABLE MAN AND OTHER STORIES (1957)
         BEYOND LIES THE WUB / THE SHORT HAPPY LIFE OF THE BROWN
             OXFORD (1987)

A139. The Visitation (sss)
         The Berkeley Gazette 14-8-44

A140. Vulcan's Hammer (NA)
         Future #29, 1956
         Satellite #20, 8-59 {translated into French, as
             Les Marteaux de Vulcain}
         VULCAN'S HAMMER (1960) {expanded}
         6 AND THE SILENT SCREAM, Howard, Belmont, 1963

A141. War Game (ss) [based on J15] ["Diversion"]
         Galaxy 12-59; #77, 1-60 (UK);
         THE PRESERVING MACHINE AND OTHER STORIES (1969)
         THE 13 CRIMES OF SCIENCE FICTION, Asimov/Greenberg/Waugh,
             Doubleday, 1979
         LES DÉLIRES DIVERGENTS DE PHILIP K. DICK (1979) {translated
             into French by Alain Dorémieux}
         ROBOTS, ANDROIDS AND MECHANICAL ODDITIES (1984)
         THE DAYS OF PERKY PAT / THE MINORITY REPORT (1987)

A142. War Veteran (NT)
        If 3-55
        THE PRESERVING MACHINE AND OTHER STORIES (1969)
        DE ONMOGELIJKE PLANEET (1976) {translated into Dutch
                by Amos Baat, as De Oorlogs Veteraan}
        THE FATHER-THING (1987)
        SECOND VARIETY (1991) {Citadel Twilight edition only}

A143. The War with the Fnools (ss)
        Galactic Outpost (fnz) #2, Spring 1964
        Galaxy 2-69
        THE GOLDEN MAN (1980)
        THE LITTLE BLACK BOX / THE EYE OF THE SIBYL (1987)
        MEMORIA TOTALE (1990) {translated into Italian by
                Mario Galli, as Bacco, Tabacco, e... Fnools}
        WE CAN REMEMBER IT FOR YOU WHOLSESALE (1991) {Grafton
                edition only}

A144. Waterspider (NT)
        If 1-64
        THE DAYS OF PERKY PAT / THE MINORITY REPORT (1987)
        MEMORIA TOTALE (1990) {translated into Italian by
                Bianca Russo, as Pulce d'Acqua}
        INSIDE THE FUNHOUSE, Resnick, AvoNova, 1992

A145. We Can Remember It For You Wholesale (NT)
        Fantasy and Science Fiction 4-66
        BEST FROM FANTASY AND SCIENCE FICTION: 16, Ferman,
                Doubleday, 1967
        NEBULA AWARD STORIES NO. 2, Aldiss/Harrison, Doubleday,
                1967; Gollancz, 1967 (as NEBULA AWARD STORIES
                1967);
        WORLD'S BEST SCIENCE FICTION: 1967, Wollheim/Carr,
                Ace, 1967
        THE PRESERVING MACHINE AND OTHER STORIES (1969)
        IMPULS 1, Storm/Wille, Hasselbalch, 1969 {translated
                into Danish by Jannick Storm and Niels Erik
                Wille, as Vi Husker for dem Engros}
        TWENTY YEARS OF FANTASY & SCIENCE FICTION, Ferman/Mills,
                Putnam's, 1970
        ALPHA 5, Silverberg, Ballantine, 1974
        EARTH IN TRANSIT, Schwartz, Dell, 1976
        Fantasy and Science Fiction 10-79; (reprinted as
                THE MAGAZINE OF FANTASY AND SCIENCE FICTION: A THIRTY
                YEAR RETROSPECTIVE, Ferman, Doubleday, 1980)
        THE ROAD TO SCIENCE FICTION #3, Gunn, Mentor, 1979
        THE LITTLE BLACK BOX (1987)
        WE CAN REMEMBER IT FOR YOU WHOLESALE (1990)
        MEMORIA TOTALE (1990) {translated into Italian by
                Beata Della Frattina, as Memoria Totale}
        [filmed as J28, 1990]
        REEL TERROR, Wolfe, Xanadu, 1992
        REEL FUTURE, Ackerman/Stine, SFBC, 1994

A146. What the Dead Men Say (NA) ["Man with a Broken Match"]
        Worlds of Tomorrow 6-64
        UBIK (1969) {expanded and adapted}
        LES DÉLIRES DIVERGENTS DE PHILIP K. DICK (1979) {translated
                into French by Alain Dorémieux}
        THE PRESERVING MACHINE AND OTHER STORIES (1987) {not in
                Gollancz or Pan editions}
        THE DAYS OF PERKY PAT / THE MINORITY REPORT (1987)

A147. What'll We Do with Ragland Park? (NT) ["No Ordinary Guy"]
        Amazing 11-63
        The Most Thrilling SF Ever Told Summer 1969
        I HOPE I SHALL ARRIVE SOON (1985)
        THE DAYS OF PERKY PAT / THE MINORITY REPORT (1987)

A148. A World of Talent (NT) ["Two Steps Right"]
        Galaxy 10-54
        THE VARIABLE MAN AND OTHER STORIES (1957) {not in French
                or German editions}
        THE FATHER-THING (1987)
        SECOND VARIETY (1991) {Citadel Twilight edition only}

A149. The World She Wanted (ss)
        Science Fiction Quarterly 5-53; #6, 5-54 (UK);
        SECOND VARIETY (1987) {not in Citadel Twilight edition}
        WE CAN REMEMBER IT FOR YOU WHOLESALE (1990)
                {Citadel Twilight edition only}

A150. Your Appointment Will Be Yesterday (NT)
        Amazing 8-66
        COUNTER-CLOCK WORLD (1967) {expanded and adapted}
        LE LIVRE D'OR DE LA SCIENCE-FICTION PHILIP K. DICK (1979)
                {translated into French by Marcel Thaon}
        THE LITTLE BLACK BOX / THE EYE OF THE SIBYL (1987)
        WE CAN REMEMBER IT FOR YOU WHOLSESALE (1991) {Grafton
                edition only}

A151. The Zap Gun (N)
        THE ZAP GUN (1967)
        PKDS Newsletter #16, 1-88 {outline}

B. Fiction Books

B1. THE ACTS OF PAUL (synopsis for unwritten novel)
        Underwood-Miller (ph)   , -87, 3pp   {distributed as part
                of the slip-cased edition of THE COLLECTED STORIES
                OF PHILIP K. DICK}

B2. ANDEN UDGAVE [A110]
        Tangents Forlaget (hb)   , -82, 42pp,   (?; Int: Ole
                E. Petersson) {translated into Danish by Ole
                E. Petersson}

B3. THE BEST OF PHILIP K DICK [C-19: K80, A6, A107, A110, A87,
                A56, A16, A31, A23, A9, A40, A37, A111, A5, A52,
                A53, A82, A36, A27, A68, F1, G73]
        Ballantine (pb) 25359-0, 3-77, 450pp, $1.95 (DiFate); 3-78
                {distributed in UK by Futura @ £1.05}
        Garland (hb) 4208-5, -82, 450pp, $19.95 (?)

B4. BEYOND LIES THE WUB [C-25: G50, K176, K471, A119, A107, A67,
                A6, A46, A114, A24, A75, A89, A58, A95, A31, A138,
                A57, A21, A113, A10, A71, A87, A45, A86, A63, A16,
                A96, A77, G35, G73, G36]
        in THE COLLECTED STORIES OF PHILIP K. DICK (1987)
        Gollancz (hb) 04407-1, 11-88, 404pp, £12.95 [omits K176]
        Citadel Twilight (tp) 1153-2, 4-90, 404pp, $12.95 (Kevin
                Kelly) {as THE SHORT HAPPY LIFE OF THE BROWN OXFORD}
                {corrects 50-75 minor typographical errors}
                [omits K176]
        Grafton (tp) 20764-3, 5-90, 510pp, £5.99 (Chris Moore)
                [omits K176]

  - BLADE RUNNER {see under DO ANDROIDS DREAM OF ELECTRIC SHEEP?}

B5. THE BOOK OF PHILIP K. DICK [C-9: A77, A134, A24, A1, A101,
                A17, A94, A9, A112]
        DAW (pb) #44, 2-73, 187pp, 95c (Karel Thole)
        Coronet (pb) 21829-0, 7-77, 189pp, 80p (?); {as THE TURNING
                WHEEL AND OTHER STORIES}
        [see also M28]
        Fanucci (pb)   , -90, 328pp, LL15000 (?) {translated into
                Italian by Maurizio Nati and Sandro Pergameno, as
                I DIFENSORI DELLA TERRA. ATTO DI FORZA}

B6. THE BROKEN BUBBLE ["The Broken Bubble of Thisbe Holt"]
    Arbor House (hb) 012-8, 7-88, 246pp, $16.95 (Powers)
    Ultramarine (hb)   , -88, 246pp, $150.00 (?) [+K68, K308]
        {limited to 124 copies, bound in half leather,
        signed by Tim Powers & James Blaylock, and bound
        with signatures from Dick's cancelled cheques}
    Ultramarine (hb)   , -88, 246pp, $325.00 (?) [+K68, K308]
        {limited to 26 copies, bound in full leather,
        signed by Tim Powers & James Blaylock, and bound
        with signatures from Dick's cancelled cheques}
    Gollancz (hb) 04434-9, 7-89, 246pp, £12.95 (Richard Jones)
    Paladin (tp) 09066-5, 8-91, 246pp, £4.99 (Chris Moore)

B7. CLANS OF THE ALPHANE MOON [derived in part from A112]
    Ace (pb) F-309, 11-64, 189pp, 40c (Valigursky);
        11036, -72, 75c (?);
    Albin Michel (pb) SF18, -73 {translated into French by
        François Truchard, as LES CLANS DE LA LUNE ALPHAINE}
    Panther (pb) 04159-1, 3-75, 205pp, 50p (Peter Jones);
        10-76, 50p (?); ?, £2.50 (?);
    J'Ai Lu (pb) 879, -78, 252pp {translated into French by
        François Truchard, as LES CLANS DE LA LUNE ALPHAINE}
    Gregg Press (hb) 2598-6, 11-79, 192pp, $12.95 [+K350]
    Dell (pb) 11084, 1-80, 251pp, $1.95 (Richard Courtney)
    Bluejay (tp) 94051-3, 7-84, 269pp, $6.95 (Barclay Shaw)
        [+K264];
    Carroll & Graf (pb) 436-5, 11-88, 269pp, $3.95 (Shaw);
        -93 (3rd); [+K264]
    Fanucci (pb)   , -91, 228pp, LL22000 (?) {translated into
        Italian by Matteo Puggioni & Gianni Pilo, as
        FOLLIA PER SETTE CLAN}
    Meulenhof (pb)   {translated into Dutch, as ZEVEN CLANS
        VAN DE ALPHAANSE MAAN}

B8. THE COLLECTED STORIES OF PHILIP K. DICK [C-5: B4, B54, B22,
        B13, B33]
    Underwood-Miller (hb)   , 5-87, 404+393+376+380+395pp
        [adds B1] {limited to 3 slip-cased copies,
        quarterbound in calfskin, with tipped in Dick
        signatures}
    Underwood-Miller (hb) 053-3, 5-87, 404+393+376+380+395pp,
        $350.00 [adds B1] {limited to 100 numbered,
        slip-cased, copies bound with signatures from
        Dick's cheques}
    Underwood-Miller (hb) 053-3, 5-87, 404+393+376+380+395pp,
        $160.00 [adds B1] {limited to 505 numbered,
        slip-cased, copies}
    Underwood-Miller (hb) 053-3, 5-87, 404+393+376+380+395pp,
        $125.00 {limited to 800 copies};
        -88, $125.00 {limited to 300 copies};
        -91, $150.00;

B9. CONFESSIONS OF A CRAP ARTIST [incl K440] ["A Chronicle of
        Verified Scientific Fact", "A Chronicle of
        Authenticated Scientific Fact by One in the Know"]
    Entwhistle (hb) 2-7, -75, 171pp, $25.00 (90 numbered
        copies, signed by Dick)
    Entwhistle (hb) 2-7, -75, 171pp, $10.00 (410 copies)
    Entwhistle (tp) 2-7, -75, 171pp, $5.95 (Richard Powers)
        (500 copies); 6-78, $3.95 (Cronan) (5000 copies);
    Laffont , -78, 314pp, FF45 {translated into French by
        Janine Herisson, as CONFESSIONS D'UN BARJO}
    Magnum (pb) 04290-6, 9-79, 172pp, 95p (Claydon, Hook & Mann)
    Timescape (pb) 44213-9, 8-82, 207pp, $2.75 (Lundgren)
    Paladin (tp) 08725-7, 1-89, 272pp, £4.50 (Ean Taylor)
    Vintage (tp) 74114-3, 7-92, 246pp, $10.00 (Heidi North)
    [filmed as J5, 1992]

B10. THE COSMIC PUPPETS [exp from A42]
    Ace (pb) D-249, 10-57, 127pp, 35c (Valigursky) // SARGASSO
        OF SPACE by Andrew North
    in I Romanzi di Urania #280, 1962 {translated into Italian
        by Luciana Piccolo Cattozzo, as LA CITTÁ SOSTITUITA}
    Berkley (pb) 06276-7, 10-83, 186pp, $2.50 (Heffernan);
    Granada (pb) 06331-5, 8-85, 143pp, £1.95 (Stephen Crisp);
    Severn House (hb) 1356-0, 11-86, 143pp, £8.50 (Nigel Hills)
    Grafton (pb) 06331-5, 3-87, 143pp, £2.50 (Crisp) (dated 1986);

B11. COUNTER-CLOCK WORLD [derived from from A150] ["The Dead
        Grow Young" / "The Dead Are Young"]
    Berkley (pb) X1372, 2-67, 160pp, 60c (Hoot);
        02568-3, 5-74, 95c (Lehr);
    Sphere (pb) 2956-4, 6-68, 160pp, 5/- (David Davies);
    Club de Livre d'Anticipation (pb) 15, -68 {translated
        into French by Michel Deutsch, as A REBROUSSE-TEMPS}
        // EN ATTENDANT L'ANNÉE DERNIÈRE
    Dall'Oglio (hb) , -72, , LL2000 {translated into
        Italian by Maria Silva, as REDIVIVI S.P.A.}
    J'Ai Lu (pb) 613, -75   {translated into French by
        Michel Deutsch, as A REBROUSSE-TEMPS}
    White Lion (hb) 199-9, -77, 160pp, £3.25 (?);
    Coronet (pb) 21830-4, 7-77, 158pp, 70p (?)
    Gregg Press (hb) 2485-8, 4-79, 160pp, $11.95 [+K187]
    Grafton (pb) 20970-0, 10-90, 236pp, £3.50 (Chris Moore)

B12. THE CRACK IN SPACE [derived from from A12 & A120]
     Ace (pb) F-377, 2-66, 190pp, 40c (Jerome Podwil);
          12126, -74, 95c (?);
     in A PHILIP K. DICK OMNIBUS (1970)
     Bibliotheque Marabout (pb) 477, -74   {translated into
          French by Christian Meistermann, as BRÈCHE DANS
          L'ESPACE}
     Magnum (pb) 36530-1, 1-77, 188pp, 70p (?);
          05830-6, 9-80, £1.10 (Chris Moore);
     in SCIENCE FICTION OMNIBUS, Bruna/Zoon, Bruna, 1981
          {translated into Dutch by Peter Cuijpers,
          as SCHEUR IN DE RUIMTE}
     Severn House (hb) 1781-7, 8-89, 188pp, £10.95 (Martin Buchan)

B13. THE DAYS OF PERKY PAT [C-18: K405, A5, A111, A13, A74, A72,
          A104, A135, A32, A141, A53, A79, A144, A146, A84,
          A23, A120, A147, A82, G73, G6, G65]
     in THE COLLECTED STORIES OF PHILIP K. DICK (1987)
     Gollancz (hb) 04756-9, 4-90, 380pp, £14.95
     Grafton (tp) 20768-6, 5-91, 494pp, £5.99 (Chris Moore)
     Citadel Twilight (tp) 1276-8, 12-91, 380pp, $12.95 (?)
          {as THE MINORITY REPORT}

B14. DÉDALES DÉMESURÉS DE PHILIP K. DICK [C-8: A66, A111,
          A78, A43, & 4 others] {edited by Alain Dorémieux}
     Casterman (pb) 33, -82, , FF52   {translated into French
          by Alain Dorémieux & Jean-Pierre Pugi}

B15. LES DÉLIRES DIVERGENTS DE PHILIP K. DICK [C-10: A107, A57,
          A20, A13, A141, A146, A92, A105, A106, A93] {edited
          by Alain Dorémieux}
          Casterman (hb) 25, -79, 240pp   {translated into French
          by Alain Dorémieux}

B16. DEUS IRAE {with Roger Zelazny} [derived in part from A45 and
          A91] ["The Kneeling Legless Man"]
     Doubleday (hb) 04527-1, 7-76, 182pp, $5.95 (John Cayea)
     Gollancz (hb) 02307-4, 6-77, 182pp, £3.75 (?);
     Dell (pb) 11838-7, 9-77, 238pp, $1.75 (Richard Courtney);
          2-78; 10-80, $2.25 (?);
     Presence du Futur (pb) 238, -77, 256pp,   {translated
          into French by Françoise Cartano}
     UKSFBC (hb)   , 3-78
     Sphere (pb) 2964-5, 7-78, 220pp, 95p (?);
          2983-1, 7-79, 95p (?); -85, £1.50 (?);
          5-88, £2.99 (Gudynas);
     Bruna SF (pb) 9082-6, -78, 237pp   (Karel Thole)
          {translated into Dutch by Annemarie Kindt, as DE
          GOD DER GRAMSCHAP}
     DAW (pb) 887-2 (#559), 12-83, 192pp, $2.95 (Bob Pepper);
     Collier Nucleus (tp) 031589-9, 9-93, 182pp, $8.00 (Terry Miura)

B17. THE DIVINE INVASION [incl A14] ["VALIS Regained"]
     Timescape (hb) 41776-2, 6-81, 239pp, $12.95 (Rowena Morrill);
     SFBC (hb) 5941, -81,   , $5.98 (Morrill);
     Corgi (pb) 11893-1, 2-82, 243pp, £1.50 (?); [+K4]
     Timescape (pb) 44343-7, 7-82, 223pp, $2.95 (Morrill);
     Presence du Futur (pb) 338, -82, , FF32 {translated
          into French by Alain Doremieux, as L'INVASION DIVINE}
     Grafton (pb) 20439-3, 5-89, 270pp, £2.99 (Chris Foss);
     in THE VALIS TRILOGY (1989)
     Vintage (tp) 73445-7, 7-91, 238pp, $10.00 (Douglas Struthers)

B18. DO ANDROIDS DREAM OF ELECTRIC SHEEP? [derived in part from
          A66] ["The Electric Toad" / "Do Androids Dream?" /
          "The Electric Sheep" / "The Killers Are Among Us!
          Cried Rick Deckard to the Special Man"]
     Doubleday (hb) 68-11779, 3-68, 210pp, $3.95 (Harry Sehring);
     Signet (pb) T3800, 3-69, 159pp, 75c (Graham?);
          T4758, -71, 75c (?);
     Rapp & Whiting (hb) 081-2, 3-69, 192pp, 21/- (Lawrence Edwards)
     Panther (pb) 03605-9, 9-72, 183pp, 30p (?);
     Notabene (pb)   , -73, 220pp,   {translated into Danish
          by Jannick Storm, as DROMMER ANDROIDER OM
          ELEKTRISKE FÅR?}
     Champ Libre (pb) 15, -76 {translated into French, as
          ROBOT BLUES}
     Granada (pb) 03605-9, 12-77, 183pp, 75p (Peter Goodfellow);
          8-82, £1.50 (movie poster);
     Titres/SF (pb) 15, -79, 256pp {translated into French, as
          LES ANDROIDÉS RÊVENT-ILS DE MOUTONS ÉLECTRIQUES}
     Del Rey (pb) 30129-3, 5-82, 216pp, $2.75 (movie poster by
          Alvin) {as BLADE RUNNER}
     [filmed as J1, 1982]
     Grafton (pb) 03605-9, -84, 183pp, £1.25 (?);
          -86, £1.95 (film collage); -87;
          -88, £2.95 (collage); -92, £3.99 (collage) (10th);
     in InterPress Magazin 4-84 & 5-84 {translated into Hungarian
          by Gálvölgyi Judit, as AZ ELEKTROMOS BÁRÁNY}
     in Nova Fantastyka #133, 10-93 & #134, 11-93 & #135, 12-93 &
          #136, 1-94 {translated into Polish}
     Meulenhof (pb)   {translated into Dutch, as DROMEN
          ANDROIDEN VAN ELEKTRICHE SHAPEN?]

B19. DR. BLOODMONEY OR HOW WE GOT ALONG AFTER THE BOMB ["In
          Earth's Diurnal Course" / "A Terran Odyssey"]
          [ext published as A127]
     Ace (pb) F-337, 6-65, 222pp, 40c (Gaughan);
          15670, -76, $1.50 (Pepper?);
     Prisma (pb) 1382, -69, 217pp,   (?) {translated into Dutch
          by Iet Houwer, as DR BLUTHGELD, LEVEN NA DE BOM}
     Club de Livre d'Anticipation (hb) 24, -70,   , FF36
          {translated into French by Bruno Martin, as
          DOCTEUR BLOODMONEY} // LE MAÎTRE DU HAUT CHÂTEAU
     J'Ai Lu (pb) 563, -74 {translated into French by Bruno
          Martin, as DOCTEUR BLOODMONEY}
     Gregg Press (hb) 2365-7, 6-77, 222pp, $11.00 [+K365]
     Arrow (pb) 914960-5, 10-77, 290pp, 80p (Peter Elson);
          9-87, £2.50 (?);
     Dell (pb) 11489, 8-80, 304pp, $2.25 (Richard Courtney);
          [+G2]
     Bluejay (tp) 94105-6, 5-85, 314pp, $7.95 (Barclay Shaw);
          [+K156 & G2]
     Carroll & Graf (pb) 389-X, 7-88, 304pp, $3.95 (?);
          [+K156 & G2]
     Edhasa (pb)   , -88, 335pp, 1300ptas (?) {translated into
          Spanish by Rubén Masera, as EL DOCTEUR
          MONEDASANGRIENTA}
     Legend (pb) 914960-5, 4-90, 290pp, £3.99 (?)

B20. DR. FUTURITY [exp from A129]
     Ace (pb) D-421, 2-60, 138pp, 35c (Valigursky) // SLAVERS
          OF SPACE by John Brunner
     in Galassia #30, 1963 {translated into Italian by
          L. Pollini, as IL DOTTOR FUTURO}
     in A PHILIP K. DICK OMNIBUS (1970)
     Ace (pb) 15697, 9-72, 172pp, 95c (Bergman) //
          THE UNTELEPORTED MAN
     Le Masque Science-Fiction (pb) 2, -74   {translated into
          French by Florian Robinet, as LE VOYAGEUR DE
          L'INCONNU}
     Methuen (pb) 36540-9, 8-76, 157pp, 60p (?);
     Magnum (pb) 04610-3, 8-79, 157pp, 85p (Chris Moore);
     Berkley (pb) 07106-5, 8-84, 153pp, $2.50 (Warhola);

B21. EYE IN THE SKY ["With Opened Mind"]
        Ace (pb) D-211,   -57, 255pp, 35c (Valigursky);
              H-39,   -68, 60c (Kelly Freas);
              22385,   -70, 95c (?);
              22386, 3-75, $1.25 (Harry Bennett);
              22387,   -77, $1.50 (?);
        Editions Satellite ,   -58 {translated into French by
              Gérard Klein, as L'OEIL DANS LE CIEL} [+K224]
        Hayakawa Shobo (pb) 3012,   -59,   , ¥200 {translated
              into Japanese by Nakada Koji, as UCHO NO ME}
        Les Cahiers de la Science Fiction (pb) 7,   -59,   , FF4.50
              {translated into French, as LES MONDES DIVERGENTS}
        in I Romanzi di Urania #201, 1959 {translated into Italian
              by Beata Della Frattina, as L'OCCHIO NEL CIELO}
        Hasselbalch (pb)   ,   -68, 208pp, Kr9.85 {translated into
              Danish by Niels Erik Wille, as ØJET PÅ HIMLEN}
        in I Romanzi di Urania #525, 1969 {translated into Italian
              by Beata Della Frattina, as L'OCCHIO NEL CIELO}
        Arrow (pb) 005100-9, 8-71, 256pp, 30p (?);
              920760-5,   -79, 95p (?); 3-87, £2.50 (?);
        Ailleurs et Demain Classiques (pb) 10,   -76 {translated
              into French by Gérard Klein, as L'OEIL DANS LE
              CIEL} [+K224]
        Gregg Press (hb) 2481-5, 11-79, 255pp, $14.95 [+K271]
        J'Ai Lu (pb) 1209,   -81 {translated into French, as
              L'OEIL DANS LE CIEL}
        Collier Nucleus (pb) 031590-2, 10-89, 255pp, $4.50 (?);
        Legend (pb) 920760-5, 3-91, 256pp, £3.99 (Peter Andrew Jones)
        Collier Nucleus (tp) 031591-0, 5-93, 243pp, $9.00 (Ron Walotsky)

   - THE EYE OF THE SIBYL {see under THE LITTLE BLACK BOX}

B22. THE FATHER-THING [C-23: K78, A35, A48, A34, A43, A134, A65,
              A37, A122, A131, A80, A132, A29, A20, A108, A112,
              A137, A40, A88, A142, A15, A73, A148, A101, G73, G64]
        in THE COLLECTED STORIES OF PHILIP K. DICK (1987)
        Gollancz (hb) 04616-3, 11-89, 376pp, £13.95
        Grafton (tp) 20767-8, 11-90, 476pp, £5.99 (Chris Moore)
        Citadel Twilight (tp) 1226-1, 6-91, 414pp, $12.95 (Kevin
              Kelly) {as SECOND VARIETY} [adds A110]

B23. FLOW MY TEARS, THE POLICEMAN SAID [unpublished ext as A26]
     Doubleday (hb) 00887-2,   -74, 231pp, $6.95
             (One Plus One);   -74;
     Gollancz (hb) 01880-1, 10-74, 231pp, £2.20 (?);
     DAW (pb) UW1166 (#146), 4-75, 208pp, $1.50 (Osterwalder);
             UW1266, 11-76, $1.50 (Kresek);   -78;
             UE1624 (#438), 6-81, $2.25 (Oliviero Berni) (5th);
             969-0,   -84, $£2.50 (?);
     UKSFBC (hb)   , 11-75, 231pp
     Le Masque Science-Fiction (pb) 22,   -75   {translated into
             French by Michel Deutsch, as LE PRISME DU NÉANT}
             [incl A26]
     Panther (pb) 04203-2, 10-76, 204pp, 60p (Richard Clifton-Dey);
             -79, 80p (?);   -84;
     Notabene (hb)   ,   -84, 171pp   {translated into Danish
             by Jannick Storm, as STRØM MINE TÅRER, SAGDE
             POLITIMANDEN}
     extract in Limbo (fnz) #5   {translated into Danish
             by Jannick Storm, as STRØM MINE TÅRER, SAGDE
             POLITIMANDEN}
     Laffont (pb)   ,   -85 {translated into French, as COULEZ
             MES LARMES, DIT LE POLICIER} [incl A26]
     [dramatized as J10, 1985]
     Grafton (pb) 04203-2,   -86, 204pp, 2.50 (?)
     Vintage (tp) 74066-X, 7-93, 231pp, $10.00 (Mikio Ishizaki)

B24. GALACTIC POT-HEALER
     Berkley (pb) X1705, 5-69, 144pp, 60c (Kossut);
             02569-1,   -74, 95c (?);
     SFBC (hb)   , 4-70,   , $1.49 (Kossut)
     Gollancz (hb) 00596-3, 7-71, 191pp, £1.60 (?);
     Pan (pb) 23337-8, 10-72, 156pp, 25p (Ian Miller);
             2-77, 60p (?);
     Titres/SF (pb) 19,   -77, 192pp   {translated into French,
             as MANQUE DE POT!}
     Presses-Pocket (pb) 5083,   -80   {translated into French,
             as LE GUÉRISSEUR DE CATHÉDRALES}
     Grafton (pb) 06937-2, 3-87, 189pp, £2.50 (Gino d'Achille);
     Vintage (tp) 75297-8, 6-94, 177pp, $9.00 (?)

B25. THE GAME-PLAYERS OF TITAN
    Ace (pb) F-251, 12-63, 191pp, 40c (Jack Gaughan);
        27310,   -72, 75c (Harry Bennett);
    Nebula (pb) 106,   -65 {translated into Spanish by
        Francisco Carzoria Olmo, as TORNEO MORTAL}
    Sphere (pb) 2957-2, 5-69, 157pp, 5/- (?);
        2959-9, 3-73, 30p (?); 2961-0, 6-77, 65p (?); 7-78;
    White Lion (hb) 577-3, 6-74, 188pp, £1.80 (?);
    Meulenhof (pb) 0267-0,   -74, 188pp,   (?) {translated into
        Dutch by David Markus, as DE SPELERS VAN TITAN}
    Le Masque Science-Fiction (pb) 74,   -78, 252pp,
        {translated into French by Maxime Barrieri,
        as LES JOUEURS DE TITAN}
    Gregg Press (hb) 2482-3, 4-79, 191pp, $13.95 [+K402]
    Grafton (pb) 20971-9, 2-91, 223pp, £3.50 (Chris Moore)
    Vintage (tp) 74065-1, 7-92, 215pp, $10.00 (?)

B26. THE GANYMEDE TAKEOVER {with Ray Faraday Nelson} ["The
        Stones Rejected"]
    Ace (pb) G-637, 6-67, 157pp, 50c (Jack Gaughan);
        27346,   -77, $1.50 (?);
    Arrow (pb) 005370-2, -71, 192pp, 25p (photo collage);
        921490-3, 2-80, 95p (?); 9-87, £2.50 (?);
    J'Ai Lu (pb) 1067,   -80, 224pp {translated into French, as
        LES MACHINES À ILLUSIONS}
    Severn House (hb) 1687-X, 12-88, 192pp, £10.95 (John
        Costelloe)
    Legend (pb) 921490-3, 3-91, 192pp, £3.99 (Peter Andrew Jones)
    Mondadori (pb)   ,   -91, 176pp, LL6000 (Oscar Chichoni)
        {translated into Italian by Luciana Agnoli Zucchini,
        as L'ORA DEI GRANDI VERMI}

B27. GATHER YOURSELVES TOGETHER [incl K75]
    WCS Books (hb) 05-7, 6-94, 291pp, $40.00 (James Kibo Parry)

B28. THE GOLDEN MAN [C-15: K196, F17, A43, A106, A63, A74,
        A78, A66, A135, A143, A65, A71, A41, A108, A92,
        A116, A93, G3, G73]
    Berkley (pb) 04288-X, 2-80, 337pp, $2.25 (Walter Velez);
    SFBC (hb) 4017, 9-80, 326pp, $5.98 (Barr);
    Magnum (pb) 06200-1, 6-81, 336pp, £1.50 (Chris Moore);
        ?, £2.50 (?);
    in I Romanzi di Urania #896, 1981 & #897, 1981
        {translated into Italian by Delio Zinoni, as
        NON SAREMO NOI and PICCOLO CITTÀ}
    J'Ai Lu (pb) 1291, -82,   , FF13 {translated into French
        by Alain Dorémieux, as L'HOMME DORÉ} [C-10:]

B29. A HANDFUL OF DARKNESS [C-15: A16, A56, A31, A91, A100, A10,
        A67, A95, A55, A57, A134, A97, A137, A18, A29]
    Rich & Cowan (hb)   , 8-55, 216pp, 10/6d (Rudland);
        6-57, 6/6d (?);
    Panther (pb) 2108, -66, 186pp, 6/- (?);
        04804-9, 1-80, 95p (Colin Hay); [omits A67, A95]
    Bruna SF (pb) 1100, -69, 189pp   (Dick Bruna) {translated
        into Dutch by Henk Bouwman, as EEN HANDVOL DUISTERNIS}
        [omits A100, A67, A95, A57, A134, A29; adds A110]
    Stig Vendelkaer (pb)   , -73, 207pp {translated into
        Danish by Kristian Kliim, as EN HÅNDFULD MØRKE}
    Terra Sonderband (pb) 76, -73 {translated into German, as
        EINE HANDVOLL DUNKELHEIT}
    Gregg Press (hb) 2413-0, 6-78, 223pp, $11.00 [+K253]
    Grafton (pb) 04804-9, 11-88, 237pp, £2.99 (Foss);
        [omits A67, A95]
    Delta SF   ,   ,   , Hft50 (?) {translated into Swedish,
        as EN HANDFULL MÖRKER}

B30. HUMPTY DUMPTY IN OAKLAND
    Gollancz (hb) 03875-6, 10-86, 199pp, £9.95 (Mark Foreman);
    Paladin (tp) 08670-6, 5-88, 199pp, £3.95 (Ean Taylor);

B31. I HOPE I SHALL ARRIVE SOON [C-10: F12, A113, A32, A50, A147,
        A123, A2, A30, A14, A103, A54]
    Doubleday (hb) 19567-2, 7-85, 179pp, $12.95 (Cathy Canzani);
    Gollancz (hb) 03578-1, 2-86, 179pp, £8.95 (?);
    St. Martin's (pb) 90838-5, 9-87, 201pp, $3.50 (Lehr?);
    Grafton (pb) 07415-5, 2-88, 220pp, £2.95 (Foss);

B32. IN MILTON LUMKY TERRITORY
    Dragon Press (hb)   , 6-85, 213pp, $150.00
            {limited to 50 copies, quarterbound in leather,
            with a pasted-in Dick signature}
    Dragon Press (hb) 09-1, 6-85, 213pp, $29.95 (Barclay Shaw)
            {limited to 950 copies}
    Gollancz (hb) 03625-7, 10-85, 213pp, £8.95 (?);
    Paladin (tp) 08602-1, 2-87, 213pp, £3.95 (Neil Breedon);

  - LIES, INC. {see under THE UNTELEPORTED MAN}

B33. THE LITTLE BLACK BOX [C-25: K119, A66, A143, A41, A92, A105,
           A127, A150, A50, A145, A78, A106, A36, A121, A27,
           A11, A68, A93, A33, A22, A30, A14, A123, A54, A103,
           A2, G73, G4, G5, F1]
     in THE COLLECTED STORIES OF PHILIP K. DICK (1987)
     Gollancz (hb) 04845-X, 10-90, 395pp, £14.95
     Grafton (tp) 20769-4, 11-91, 495pp, £5.99 (Chris Moore)
           {as WE CAN REMEMBER IT FOR YOU WHOLESALE}
     Citadel Twilight (tp) 1328-4, 5-92, 395pp, $12.95 (Kevin
           Kelly) {as THE EYE OF THE SIBYL} [omits A145]

B34. LE LIVRE D'OR DE LA SCIENCE-FICTION PHILIP K. DICK
           [C-12: K398, A88, A55, A52, A116, A17, A41, A112,
           A104, A73, A150, A120, A23, K396] {edited by
           Marcel Thaon}
     Presses-Pocket (pb) 5051, -79, 360pp   {translated into
           French by Marcel Thaon}

B35. THE MAN IN THE HIGH CASTLE
     Putnams (hb) 62-18262, 10-62, 239pp, $3.95 (Robert Galster)
           {distributed in Canada by Longmans};
     SFBC (hb)   , 11-62, 218pp, $1.20 (Galster);
           3686, 3-80, $3.50 (Tony Gleeson);
     Popular Library (pb) SP250, 1-64, 191pp, 50c (?);
           60-2289, -68, 60c (?);
     Penguin (pb) 002376-3, -65, 236pp, 5/- (Max Ernst);
           4-76, 60p (Peter Goodfellow);
           11-78, 75p (Goodfellow); 9-86;
     Club de Livre d'Anticipation (hb) 24, -70, , FF36
           {translated into French by Bruno Martin, as
           LE MAÎTRE DU HAUT CHÂTEAU} // DOCTEUR BLOODMONEY
     Stig Vendelkaer (pb)   , -73, 228pp,   {translated into
           Danish by Jørgen Beck-Jessen, as MANDEN I DEN
           STORE FÆSTNING}
     Berkley (pb) Z2543, 4-74, 253pp, $1.25 (Richard M. Powers);
           03080, -74, $1.50 (?); 03908, -78, $1.75 (Powers);
           04323, -79, $1.95 (?); 05051, 3-81, $2.25 (?) (9th);
           06321-6, 12-83, $2.50 (?); 10143-6, 12-84, $2.95 (?);
     J'Ai Lu (pb) 567, -74 {translated into French by Jacques
           Parsons, as LE MAÎTRE DU HAUT CHÂTEAU}
     Gollancz (hb) 01958-1, 5-75, 222pp, £3.20 (?)
     UKSFBC (hb)   , 3-76, 222pp
     Gregg Press (hb) 2476-9, 4-79, 239pp, $9.95 [+K272]
     Penguin (tp) 008875-X, 3-87, 249pp, £3.95 (Fred Gambino);
     Easton Press (hb)   , 3-88, 239pp   (int: Richard Powers)
     Vintage (tp) 74067-8, 7-92, 259pp, $10.00 (?)

B36. THE MAN WHO JAPED
        Ace (pb) D-193, 12-56, 160pp, 35c (Emsh) // SPACE-BORN by
                E.C. Tubb
        Cenit (pb) 6, -60 {translated into Spanish, as
                PLANETAS MORALES}
        Ace (pb) 51910, -75, 160pp, 95c (Dean Ellis);
        Sagittaire (pb) 8, -77, 254pp   {translated into French
                by Phillippe Lorrain & Baudouin Panloup, as LE
                DÉTOURNEUR}
        Eyre Methuen (hb) 39290-2, 10-78, 158pp, £3.50 (Chris Moore);
        Magnum (pb) 02590-4, 10-78, 158pp, 85p (Chris Moore);   -83;
        Bruna SF (pb) 1993-8, -81, 160pp, Bfr105 (Peter Andrew Jones)
                {translated into Dutch by Henk Bouwman, as
                DE LAATSTE LACH}
        Methuen (pb) 02590-4, -87, 158pp, £2.95 (Richard Sparks);

B37. THE MAN WHOSE TEETH WERE ALL EXACTLY ALIKE [incl K439]
        Zeising (hb) 0-X, 6-84, 223pp, $15.95 (Dell Harris)
                {limited to 800 copies}
        Ziesing (tp) 5-0, 2-86, 223pp, $9.95 (Dell Harris)
                {limited to 3000 copies}
        Paladin (tp) 08563-7, 8-86, 256pp, £2.95 (Neil Breedon);

B38. MARTIAN TIME-SLIP [exp from A4] ["Goodmember Arnie Kott
                of Mars"]
        Ballantine (pb) U2191, 4-64, 220pp, 50c (Brillhart);
                25224, -76, $1.50 (Darrell Sweet);
        [televised as J17, 1960s]
        Meulenhof (pb) 0328-6, -74, 243pp,   (Chris Foss)
                {translated into Dutch by Parma Van Loon, as
                MARTIAANSE TIJDSVERSCHUIVING}
        NEL (hb) 02978-6, 6-76, 240pp, £3.95 (Gerald Grace); [+K41]
        NEL (pb) 03001-6, 3-77, 240pp, 90p (Bruce Pennington);
                7-83, £1.75 (?); [+K41]
        Del Rey (pb) 29560, 6-81, 220pp, $2.25 (Sweet) (4th);
                34444, -89, ? (7th); -90;
        Ailleurs et Demain Classiques (pb) 18, -81 {translated
                into French, as GLISEMENT DE TEMPS SUR MARS}
        [staged as J18, 1987]
        Gollancz (pb) 04710-0, 5-90, 220pp, £3.50 (?)

B39. MARY AND THE GIANT
        Arbor House (hb) 850-5, 3-87, 230pp, $16.95 (Richard Powers);
        Ultramarine Press (hb)   , -87, 230pp, $150.00 {limited to
                50 copies, quarterbound in leather, with a
                tipped-in Dick signature}
        Gollancz (hb) 04243-5, 2-88, 240pp, £10.95 (?)
        Paladin (tp) 08783-4, 8-89, 220pp, £4.99 (Ean Taylor)
        St. Martin's (tp) 03398-2, 10-89, 230pp, $8.95 (Vincent Kirsch)

B40. A MAZE OF DEATH [incl G7] ["The Name of the Game is Death"]
     Doubleday (hb) 70-111158, 7-70, 216pp, $4.95 (Michelle
          Moschella)
     Paperback Library (pb) 64-636, 7-71, 190pp, 75c (Powers);
     Gollancz (hb) 00694-3, 1-72, 216pp, £1.80 (?);
     Ailleurs et Demain (pb) 19, -72 {translated into French
          by Alain Dorémieux, as AU BOUT DU LABYRINTHE}
     Prisma (pb) 0644-8, -72, 175pp, (Studio Spectrum)
          {translated into Dutch by G.R.Chr.M. Suurmeijer,
          as VLUCHT IN VISIOENEN}
     Pan (pb) 23769-1, 11-73, 190pp, 35p (Ian Miller);
          2-77, 60p (?);
     Bantam (pb) 10740-2, 9-77, 182pp, $1.75 (Szafran);
     J'Ai Lu (pb) 774, -77, 224pp {translated into French
          by Alain Dorémieux, as AU BOUT DU LABYRINTHE}
     DAW (pb) 830-9 (#533), 6-83, 191pp, $2.50 (?)
     Grafton (pb) 05897-4, 5-84, 191pp, £1.50 (Tim Gill);
          2-87, £2.50 (Gill); 8-92, £4.99 (Chris Moore);
     Móra Kiadó (tp) 698-4, -86, 207pp, 33ft (Korga György)
          {translated into Hungarian by Veres Mihály, as
          A HALÁL ÚTVESZTŐJE]
     Vintage (UK) 75298-6, 6-94, 192pp, $10.00 (?)

B41. MEMORIA TOTALE [C-11: A67, A17, A16, A110, A72, A144, A92
          A50, A145, A143, A27]
     Altri Mondi (pb) , -90, 262pp, (Oscar Chichoni)
          {translated into Italian}

  - THE MINORITY REPORT {see under THE DAYS OF PERKY PAT}

B42. NICK AND THE GLIMMUNG ["The Glimmung of Plowman's Planet"]
     Gollancz (hb) 04307-5, 6-88, 141pp, £7.95 (Paul Demeyer;
          Int: Demeyer);
     Piper (pb) 31474-2, 7-90, 141pp, £2.50 (Demeyer; Int: Demeyer)

B43. NOW WAIT FOR LAST YEAR
     Doubleday (hb) 66-017393, 5-66, 214pp, $3.95 (Lawrence
          Ratzkin) {some copies distributed by the SFBC
          in 2-68 for $1.95}
     Macfadden (pb) 00352, -68, 224pp, 60c (photo)
     Club de Livre d'Anticipation (pb) 15, -68 {translated
          into French by Michel Deutsch, as EN ATTENDANT
          L'ANNÉE DERNIÈRE} // A REBROUSSE-TEMPS
     Le Livre de Poche SF (pb) 7000, -77, 352pp, FF31 (?);
          -87 (5th); {translated into French, as
          EN ATTENDANT L'ANNÉE DERNIÈRE}
     Manor (pb) 12-214, 5-74, 224pp, $1.25 (?);
          12410, -76, $1.25 (?);
     Panther (pb) 04208-3, 6-75, 224pp, 50p (Chris Foss); 10-76;
          9-79, 85p (?);

B43. NOW WAIT FOR LAST YEAR (cont)
Granada (pb) 04208-3, -84, 224pp, £1.95 (Foss);
DAW (pb) 645-3 (#450), 9-81, 205pp, $2.50 (?);
Vintage (tp) 74220-4, 7-93, 230pp, $10.00 (Marco Monti)
Meulenhof (pb)   {translated into Dutch, as WACHT NU OP
        VOLGEND JAAR}

B44. DE ONMOGELIJKE PLANEET [C-9: A55, A56, A107, A88, A142,
        A6, A20, A13, A16]
Bruna & Zoon (pb) 9040-0, -76, 189pp,   (Marion Crezée)
        {translated into Dutch by Henk Bouwman & Amos Baat}

B45. OUR FRIENDS FROM FROLIX 8 [outline published as A85]
Ace (pb) 64400, 6-70, 189pp, 60c (Schoenherr); -72;
        64401-5, -77, $1.50 (David Plourde);
SFBC (hb)   , 2-71,   , $1.49 (Kim Whitesides);
Opta (pb) 4, -72 {translated into French by Robert Louit,
        as LE MESSAGE DE FROLIX 8}
Panther (pb) 04295-4, 1-76, 211pp, 60p (Jim Burns);
        10-76; -84;
Le Masque Science-Fiction (pb) 83, -78, 250pp
        {translated into French by Robert Louit,
        as LE MESSAGE DE FROLIX 8}
Grafton (pb) 04295-4, -88, 211pp, £2.95 (Jim Burns);
Kinnell (hb) 08-2, 6-89, 211pp, £11.95 (Keith Roberts)
Meulenhof (pb)   {translated into Dutch, as ONZE
        VRIENDEN VAN FROLIX 8}

B46. THE PENULTIMATE TRUTH [derived in part from A24 and A74]
Belmont (pb) 92-603, 9-64, 174pp, 50c (?);
Cape (hb) 61158-5, 6-67, 254pp, 25/- (?);
Penguin (pb) 003105-7, 5-70, 221pp, 6/- (Franco Grignani);
Ailleurs et Demain (pb) 32, -74   {translated into French
        by Alain Dorémieux, as LA VÉRITÉ AVANT-DÈRNIERE}
Leisure (pb) 285NK, -75, 174pp, 95c (photo);
Panther (pb) 04787-5, 11-78, 207pp, 95p (Peter Goodfellow);
        -84;
J'Ai Lu (pb) 910, -79   {translated into French by Alain
        Dorémieux, as LA VÉRITÉ AVANT-DÈRNIERE}
Dell (pb) 16296, 2-80, 238pp, $1.95 (Corben);
Narrativa D'Anticipazione (pb) 25, -81, 210pp
        (Michelangelo Miani) {translated into Italian by
        Mauro Cesari, as LA PENULTIMA VERITÀ}
Bluejay (tp) 94356-3, 2-84, 201pp, $5.95 (Barclay Shaw);
        [+K121]
Carroll & Graf (pb) 493-4, 6-89, 220pp, $3.95 (?) [+K121]
Triad Grafton (pb) 04787-5, -87, 240pp, £2.50 (Goodfellow)
Grafton (pb) 21030-X, 10-92, 240pp, £4.99 (Chris Moore)
Meulenhof (pb)   {translated into Dutch, as UUR VAN
        DE WAARHEID}

B47. A PHILIP K. DICK OMNIBUS [C-3: B12, B62, B20]
     Sidgwick & Jackson (hb) 48450-0, 10-70, 424pp, £1.95 (?);
     in SCIENCE FICTION SPECIAL #7, Anon, Sidgwick & Jackson,
        1973

B48. PHILIP K. DICK OMNIBUS [C-14: A97, A72, A137, A10, A111,
        A19, A9, A91, A31, A17, A23, A18, A116, A110]
        {edited by Aart C. Prins}
     Bruna (pb) 9068-0, -77, 340pp, Bfr135 (Karel Thole)
        {translated into Dutch by Henk Bouwman &
        Kees Van Den Broek}

B49. THE PRESERVING MACHINE AND OTHER STORIES [C-15: A95, A141,
        A137, A107, A142, A120, A6, A145, A13, A53, A105,
        A20, A82, A146, A88]
     Ace (pb) 67800, 4-69, 317pp, 95c (Leo & Diane Dillon);
        67801, -76, $1.95 (David Schleinkofer);
     SFBC (hb) , 1-70, , $1.69 (Leo & Diane Dillon);
     Gollancz (hb) 00562-9, 2-71, 256pp, £1.80 (?) [omits A146];
     UKSFBC (hb) 5041, 2-72
     Pan (pb) 23363-7, 11-72, 288pp, 35p (?); -77, 70p (?);
        [omits A146]
     Grafton (pb) 06938-0, 10-87, 413pp, £3.50 (Chris Foss);

B50. PUTTERING ABOUT IN A SMALL LAND [extract published as A102]
     Academy Chicago (hb) 149-4, 10-85, 291pp, $16.95 (Armen
        Kojoyian)
     Paladin (tp) 08604-8, 8-87, 286pp, £3.95 (Neil Breedon);
     Academy Chicago (tp) 384-5, 9-92, 291pp, $11.95 (Kojoyian)

B51. RADIO FREE ALBEMUTH ["Valisystem A"]
     Arbor House (hb) 762-2, 12-85, 214pp, $14.95 (Walotsky);
     SFBC (hb) 01801, 6-86, 214pp, $4.98 (Walotsky);
     Grafton (pb) 06936-4, 5-87, 286pp, £2.95 (Tony Roberts);
     Avon (pb) 70288-6, 6-87, 212pp, $3.50 (Walotsky);
        ?, $3.95 (?) (5th);
     Severn House (hb) 1537-7, 10-87, 288pp, £9.95 (?);
     [staged as J24, 1991]

B52. ROBOTS, ANDROIDS, AND MECHANICAL ODDITIES: THE SCIENCE
        FICTION OF PHILIP K. DICK [C-15: A110, A56, A111,
        A5, A27, A67, A24, A54, A95, A108, A65, A30, A132,
        A141, A41] {edited by Patricia S. Warrick &
        Martin H. Greenberg}
     Southern Illinois University Press (hb) 1159-3, 6-84,
        261pp, $19.95 (?)
     Southern Illinois University Press (tp) 1178-X, 3-86,
        261pp, $9.95 (?)

B53. A SCANNER DARKLY [incl G8]
        Doubleday (hb) 01613-1,   -77, 220pp, $6.95 (The Quay
                Brothers);
        Gollancz (hb) 02381-3, 11-77, 220pp, £3.50 (?);
        SFBC (hb) 15503,   -77, 220pp, $2.98 (The Quay Brothers);
        Del Rey (pb) 26064, 12-77, 288pp, $1.95 (Ochagavia);
        UKSFBC (hb)   , 9-78
        Granada (pb) 04553-8, 12-78, 254pp, 95p (?);   -85;
        Presence du Futur (pb) 252,   -78, 304pp   {translated into
                French by Robert Louit, as SUBSTANCE MORT}
        DAW (pb) 923-2 (#575), 4-84, 222pp, $2.50 (Pepper);
        Grafton (pb) 04553-8,   -87, 254pp, £2.50 (Trevor Webb);
        Vintage (tp) 73665-4, 12-91, 222pp, $10.00 (?)

B54. SECOND VARIETY [C-27: K366, A18, A7, A110, A61, A19, A97,
                A117, A70, A17, A149, A125, A98, A133, A9, A94,
                A51, A81, A52, A1, A55, A56, A59, A91, A116,
                A118, A126, A100, G73]
        in THE COLLECTED STORIES OF PHILIP K. DICK (1987)
        Gollancz (hb) 04460-8, 4-89, 395pp, £12.95
        Grafton (tp) 20765-1, 7-90, 493pp, £5.99 (Chris Moore)
        Citadel Twilight (tp) 1209-1, 9-90, 381pp, $12.95 (Norris
                Burroughs) {as WE CAN REMEMBER IT FOR YOU WHOLESALE}
                [omits A110; adds A145]
        see also under THE FATHER THING

  - THE SHORT HAPPY LIFE OF THE BROWN OXFORD {see under BEYOND
                LIES THE WUB}

B55. THE SIMULACRA [derived in part from A79] ["The First Lady
                of Earth"]
        Ace (pb) F-301,   -64, 192pp, 40c (Ed Emshwiller);
                76701,   -76, 246pp, $1.50 (?);
        Dimensions SF (pb) 3,   -73 {translated into French by
                Marcel Thaon & Christian Gueret, as SIMULACRES}
        J'Ai Lu (pb) 594,   -75 {translated into French by
                Marcel Thaon & Christian Gueret, as SIMULACRES}
        Magnum (pb) 01970-X, 6-77, 220pp, 75p (Chris Moore);
                ?, £2.95 (?);
        Eyre Methuen (hb) 37750-4, 7-77, 220pp, £2.95 (Chris Moore);
        Born (tp)   , -79,   , Bfr240 (?) {translated into Dutch,
                as DE NAMAAKMENS}

B56. SOLAR LOTTERY ["Quizmaster Take All"]
    Ace (pb) D-103, 5-55, 188pp, 35c (Valigursky) // THE BIG
        JUMP by Leigh Brackett
    Rich & Cowan (hb)   , 6-56, 160pp, 9/6d (?);
        12-57, 6/6d (?); {revised, as WORLD OF CHANCE}
    UKSFBC (hb) 26, 5-57,   , 4/6d (?); {Rich & Cowan text,
        as WORLD OF CHANCE}
    Abenteuer im Weltenraum (pb) 7, -58 {translated into
        German, as GRIFF NACH DER SONNE}
    Panther (pb) 785, 2-59, 156pp, 2/6d (?) {Rich & Cowan text,
        as WORLD OF CHANCE}
    Ace (pb) D-340, -59, 188pp, 35c (Valigursky);
        G-718, -68, 50c (Jack Gaughan);
        77410, -70, 50c (?);
        77411, -75, $1.25 (?);
    Cenit (pb) 4, -60 {translated into Spanish, as LOTERIA
        SOLAR}
    Terra Extra 47, -64 {translated into German, as GRIFF
        NACH DER SONNE}
    Galaxie Bis (pb) 7, -68 {translated into French, as
        LOTERIE SOLAIRE}
    Arrow (pb) 905700-X, 1-72, 188pp, 30p (CY);
        12-79, 95p (Peter Elson); 3-87, £2.50 (?);
    J'Ai Lu (pb) 547, -74; -78; {translated into French by
        Frank Straschitz, as LOTERIE SOLAIRE}
    Gregg Press (hb) 2330-4, 6-76, 188pp, $9.50 [+K123]
    Legend (pb) 905700-X, 4-90, 188pp, £3.50 (?)
    Collier Nucleus (pb) 029125-6, 4-90, 188pp, $3.95
        (Edward Soyka)
    Collier Nucleus (tp) 023621-2, 9-92, 200pp, $9.00 (Soyka)

B57. EEN SWIBBEL VOOR DAG EN NACHT [C-7: A9, A19, A111, A72, A17,
        A23, A116] {edited by Aart C. Prins}
    Bruna (pb) 1295, -69, 189pp,   (Dick Bruna) {translated
        into Dutch by C.A.G. Von Den Broek}

B58. THE THREE STIGMATA OF PALMER ELDRITCH [exp from A23]
    Doubleday (hb) 65-011537, 11-64, 278pp, $4.95 (Tom Chibbaro);
    SFBC (hb)   , 1-65, 230pp, $1.20 (Chibbaro);
        05829, 8-92, $8.98 (Ron Walotsky);
    Cape (hb)   , -66, 278pp, 21/- (Jan Pienkowski);
    Macfadden (pb) 60-240, -66, 191pp, 60c (Jack Faragasso);
        75-399, -71, 95c (?);
    Galaxie-Bis (pb) 11, -69 {translated into French, as
        LE DIEU VENU DU CENTAURE}
    Born (tp) 0282-4, -72, 221pp,   (Alex Jagtenberg)
        {translated into Dutch by H.J. Oolbekkink,
        as DE DRIE STIGMATA VAN PALMER ELDRITCH}
    Penguin (pb) 003399-8, 10-73, 203pp, 30p (?);
    Opta Anti-Mondes (pb) 12, -74 {translated into French
        by Guy Abadia, as LE DIEU VENU DU CENTAURE}
    Bantam (pb) 10586-8, 6-77, 245pp, $1.75 (Szafran);

B58. THE THREE STIGMATA OF PALMER ELDRITCH (cont)
        Manor (pb) 12296, -77, 191pp, $1.25 (?);
        Bibliotheque Marabout (pb) 617, -77 {translated into
                French, as LE DIEU VENU DU CENTAURE}
        Panther (pb) 04584-8, 11-78, 204pp, 85p (Peter Gudynas);
        Gregg Press (hb) 2479-3, 11-79, 278pp, $14.95 [+K443]
        J'ai Lu (pb) 1379, -82, , FF13 {translated into French
                by Guy Abadia, as LE DIEU VENU DU CENTAURE}
        DAW (pb) 810-4 (#523), 3-83, 192pp, $2.50 (Pepper);
        Triad Panther (pb) 04584-8, -84, 204pp, £1.95 (Gudynas);
        Triad Granada (pb) 04584-4, -87, 204pp, £2.50 (Gudynas);
        Vintage (tp) 73666-2, 12-91, 202pp, $10.00 (?)
        Grafton (pb) 21031-8, 8-92, 204pp, £4.99 (Chris Moore)

B59. TIME OUT OF JOINT [abridged as A128] ["Biography in Time"]
        Lippincott (hb) 59-7775, -59, 221pp, $3.95 (Arthur Hawkins)
                {distributed in Canada by Longmans @ C$3.95}
        UKSFBC (hb) 54, 10-61, , 5/6d (?);
        Zimmerman , -62 {translated into German, as ZEIT OHNE
                GRENZEN}
        Belmont (pb) 92-618, 2-65, 175pp, 50c (?);
                51143-6, -77, $1.25 (Doug Beekman);
        Penguin (pb) 002847-1, 10-69, 187pp, 5/- (Franco Grignani);
                4-76, 50p (Peter Tybus); -84, £1.95 (?); [+K4]
        Rapp & Whiting (hb) , -70, , 28/- (?) (possibly
                phantom?)
        Dimensions SF (pb) 17, -75, , FF29 {translated into
                French by Philippe R. Hupp, as LE TEMPS DÉSARTICULÉ}
        Le Livre de Poche (pb) 7021, -78, 317pp {translated into
                French by Philippe R. Hupp, as LE TEMPS DÉSARTICULÉ}
        Gregg Press (hb) 2480-7, 4-79, 221pp, $14.95 [+K374]
        Dell (pb) 18860, 11-79, 255pp, $2.25 (Corben);
        Bluejay (tp) 94427-6, 11-84, 263pp, $6.95 (Barclay Shaw);
                [+K374]
        Carroll & Graf (pb) 352-0, 12-87, 263pp, $3.95 (?); [+K374]
        Penguin (tp) 009632-9, 5-88, 187pp, £3.95 (Tom Simpson);

B60. THE TRANSMIGRATION OF TIMOTHY ARCHER ["Bishop Timothy Archer"]
        Timescape (hb) 44066-7, 4-82, 240pp, $15.50 (Powers);
        Gollancz (hb) 03220-0, 10-82, 254pp, £6.95 (?);
        Timescape (pb) 46571-4, 4-83, 255pp, $2.95 (Powers); [+K4]
        Panther (pb) 05886-9, 11-83, 252pp, £1.95 (George Underwood);
        [dramatized as J29, 1984]
        Grafton (pb) 05886-9, 3-87, 252pp, £2.50 (George Underwood);
        in THE VALIS TRILOGY (1989)
        Vintage (tp) 73444-9, 7-91, 253pp, $10.00 (?)

    -   THE TURNING WHEEL AND OTHER STORIES {see under THE BOOK OF
                PHILIP K. DICK}

B61. UBIK [derived from from A146] ["Death of an Anti-Watcher"]
        Doubleday (hb) 69-15205, 5-69, 202pp, $4.50 (Peter Rauch);
        SFBC (hb)   , -69
        Dell (pb) 9200, 5-70, 208pp, 95c (? Jones);
        Rapp & Whiting (hb) 164-9, 6-70, 202pp, 28/- (?);
        Ailleurs et Demain (pb) 7, -70 {translated into French by
            Alain Doremieux}
        Panther (pb) 03716-0, 5-73, 191pp, 35p (Tony Roberts);
        Notabene (pb) , -73, 220pp {translated into Danish by
            Jannick Storm}
        J'Ai Lu (pb) 633, -75 {translated into French by
            Alain Doremieux}
        Meulenhof (pb) 0310-3, -75, 220pp,   (Peter Jones)
            {translated into Dutch by Paul Griffen}
        Bantam (pb) 10402-0, 1-77, 212pp, $1.75 (Szafran);
            (2 printings)
        Granada (pb) 03716-0, 4-78, 191pp, 75p (Ian Robertson);
            -84, £1.95 (Robertson);
        Gregg Press (hb) 2478-5, 4-79, 202pp, $10.95 [+K64]
        DAW (pb) 859-7 (#546), 9-83, 176pp, $2.50 (Pepper);
        [adapted as screenplay E1, 1985]
        Grafton (pb) 03716-0, 11-88, 191pp, £2.50 (Robertson);
            10-92, £4.99 (Chris Moore);
        Vintage (tp) 73664-6, 12-91, 191pp, $10.00 (?)

B62. THE UNTELEPORTED MAN [exp from A136]
        Ace (pb) G-602, 11-66, 100pp, 50c (Kelly Freas) // THE MIND
            MONSTERS by Howard L. Cory
        in A PHILIP K. DICK OMNIBUS (1970)
        Ace (pb) 15697, 9-72, 107pp, 95c (Bergman) // DR. FUTURITY
        Methuen (pb) 36550-6, 8-76, 124pp, 50p (Chris Moore);
        Magnum (pb) 04600-6, 8-79, 124pp, 80p (?);
        Berkley (pb) 06252-X, 8-83, 202pp, $2.75 (?); {revised}
        Gollancz (hb) 03449-1, 7-84, 199pp, £7.95; {revised,
            as LIES, INC.}
        Meulenhof (pb) 1538-1, 12-84, 112pp,   (John Harris)
            {original magazine text, translated into Dutch by
            Jaime Martijn, as DE EENLING}
        Granada (pb) 06464-8, 10-85, 223pp, £1.95 (Trevor Webb);
            {revised, as LIES, INC.}

B63. VALIS ["To Scare the Dead" / "Zebra"]
     Bantam (pb) 14156-2, 2-81, 227pp, $2.25 (Berkey);
          20594, 6-81, $2.50 (Berkey);
     Corgi (pb) 11841-9, 11-81, 227pp, £1.25 (?);
     Presence du Futur (pb) 317, -81 {translated into French,
          as SIVA}
     Bantam Spectra (pb) 25370-0, 11-85, 227pp, $2.95 (?);
     Kerosina (hb) 15-X, 11-87, 256pp, £75.00 (Keith Roberts)
          [+K336, distributed with H1] {limited to 25
          copies, signed by Kim Stanley Robinson and with
          a `tipped-in' Dick signature}
     Kerosina (hb) 15-X, 11-87, 256pp, £37.50 (Keith Roberts)
          [+K336, distributed with H1] {limited to 275
          copies, signed by Kim Stanley Robinson}
     Kerosina (hb) 16-8, 11-87, 256pp, £13.95 (Keith Roberts)
          [+K336] {limited to 2200 copies}
     [adapted as opera J30, 1988]
     in THE VALIS TRILOGY (1989)
     Vintage (tp) 73446-5, 7-91, 241pp, $10.00 (?)
     Grafton (pb) 09201-3, 12-92, 271pp, £4.99 (Chris Moore)

B64. THE VALIS TRILOGY [C-3: B63, B17, B60, K336]
     QPBC (tp)   , 12-89, 752pp, $11.95 (Max Singer)
               {distributed in the UK by TSP, 3-93, @ £9.99}
     BOMC (hb) , 2-90, 752pp, $13.95 (Singer)

B65. THE VARIABLE MAN AND OTHER STORIES [C-5: A138, A110, A72,
          A5, A148]
     Ace (pb) D-261, -57, 255pp, 35c (Emsh);
          86050, -76, $1.50 (Corrikolayski);
     Cenit (pb) 14, -61 {translated into Spanish, as
          GUERRA CON CENTAURO}
     Terra (pb) 322-323, -64 {translated into German, as
          KRIEG DER AUTOMATEN} [omits A148]
     Sphere (pb) 2958-0, 8-69, 220pp, 6/- (?);
          2962-9, 9-77, 75p (?); 7-78;
     Le Masque Science-Fiction (pb) 31, -75 {translated into
          French, as L'HOMME VARIABLE} [omits A5, A148]

B66. VULCAN'S HAMMER [A140]
        Ace (pb) D-457, 9-60, 139pp, 35c (Emsh) // THE SKYNAPPERS
                by John Brunner
        Terra (pb) 395, -65   {translated into German, as
                VULKANS HAMMER}
        Ace (pb) 86608, -72, 154pp, 75c (Freas);
        Le Masque Science-Fiction (pb) 28, -75 {translated
                into French by Monique Benatre, as LES
                MARTEAUX DE VULCAIN}
        Arrow (pb) 913300-8, 8-76, 154pp, 50p (Peter Elson);
                -82, £1.25 (Elson);
        Bruna & Zoon (pb) 9090-7, -78, 192pp   (Karel Thole)
                {translated into Dutch by Elly Schurink-Vooren,
                as DE HAMER VAN DONAK}
        Gregg Press (hb) 2484-X, 11-79, 139pp, $11.95 [+K179]
        Mondadori (pb) 156, -90, 160pp, LL5000 {translated into
                Italian by Beata Della Frattina, as VULCANO 3}

B67. WE CAN BUILD YOU [serialized as A3] ["The First in Your
                Family"]
        DAW (pb) UQ1014 (#14), 7-72, 206pp, 95c (Schoenherr)
                {distributed in the UK by NEL @ 30p} [+K4];
                UY1164, 3-75, $1.25 (Eddie Jones);
                793-0, 1-83, $2.50 (Pepper);
        Champ Libre (pb) 8, -75   {translated into French by
                Georges & Anned Dutter, as LE BAL DES SCHIZOS}
        Fontana (pb) 614616-3, 5-77, 208pp, 70p (Peter Tybus)
        Titres/SF (pb) 3, -79, 320pp   {translated into French by
                Georges & Anned Dutter, as LE BAL DES SCHIZOS}
        Grafton (pb) 06490-7, 1-86, 252pp, £2.50 (Foss);
                ?, £2.95 (?);
        Severn House (hb) 1595-4, 6-88, 252pp, £9.95 (Foss);
        Vintage (tp) 75296-X, 6-94, 246pp, $10.00 (?)

B68. WE CAN REMEMBER IT FOR YOU WHOLESALE [A145]
        Dark Carnival (ph) , 7-90, 18pp, $1.00 (?)
        see also under SECOND VARIETY and THE LITTLE BLACK BOX

B69. THE WORLD JONES MADE ["Womb for Another"]
Ace(pb) D-150, 3-56, 192pp, 35c (Schulz) // AGENT OF THE
UNKNOWN by Margaret St. Clair
Abenteuer im Weltenraum (pb) 8, -58 {translated into
German, as GEHEIM PROJEKT VENUS}
Cenit (pb) 3, -60 {translated into Spanish, as
EL TIEMPO DOBLADE}
Terra Extra (pb) 73, -65 {translated into German, as
GEHEIM PROJEKT VENUS}
Ace (pb) F-429, -67, 192pp, 40c (Kelly Freas);
90951, -75, $1.25 (?);
Sidgwick & Jackson (hb) 98048-6, 8-68, 192pp, 18/- (?);
Panther (pb) 02949-4, 1-70, 160pp, 25p (?);
in SCIENCE FICTION SPECIAL #1, Anon, Sidgwick & Jackson,
1970
Sidgwick & Jackson/NEL (pb) 98364-7, 12-76, 160pp, 60p
(Terry Oakes)
Le Masque Science-Fiction (pb) 41, -76 {translated into
French, as LES CHAÎNES DE L'AVENIR}
Ridderhof (tp) 0287-1, -76, 221pp, f9.91 (Chris Foss)
{translated into Dutch by Ruud Bal, as DE
STERRENZWERVERS}
Gregg Press (hb) 2483-1, 11-79, 192pp, $12.95 [+K91]
Bart (pb) 012-7, 3-88, 192pp, $2.95 (?)
Vintage (tp) 74219-0, 7-93, 199pp, $10.00 (Ryuichi Oleano)
HarperCollins UK (pb) 21844-0, 6-94, 192pp, £4.99 (?)

- WORLD OF CHANCE {see under SOLAR LOTTERY}

B70. THE ZAP GUN [ser as A99; outline published as A151]
Pyramid (pb) R1569, 1-67, 176pp, 50c (Jack Gaughan);
Le Masque Science-Fiction (pb) 16, -74   {translated into
French by Raymond Albeck, as DEDALUS MAN}
Panther (pb) 04112-5, 2-75, 190pp, 40p (Peter Jones);
10-76, 75p (?); 6-78, 75p (Jones); ?, £1.95 (?);
Dell (pb) 19907, 8-78, 252pp, $1.75 (?);
Gregg Press (hb) 2494-7, 4-79, 176pp, $12.95 [+K302]
Bluejay (tp) 94488-8, 5-85, 258pp, $7.95 (Barclay Shaw)
[+K201]
Carroll & Graf (pb) 553-1, 9-89, 258pp, $3.95 (?);
-93 (3rd); [+K201]

C. Series

C1. Jim Briskin
The Mold of Yancy
What'll We Do with Ragland Park?
Stand-By
THE THREE STIGMATA OF PALMER ELDRITCH
THE CRACK IN SPACE

C2. VALIS
VALIS   } THE
THE DIVINE INVASION   }   VALIS
THE TRANSMIGRATION OF TIMOTHY ARCHER   }   TRILOGY
Chains of Air, Web of Aether
RADIO FREE ALBEMUTH
COSMOGONY AND COSMOLOGY
IN PURSUIT OF VALIS: SELECTIONS FROM THE EXEGESIS

D. Poems, Songs, Plays and TV/Film Scripts

D1. The Above and Melting (poem)
A CHILD'S HAT, Gulyas, 1966

D2. He's Dead (poem)
The Berkeley Gazette
TO THE HIGH CASTLE by Gregg Rickman, Fragments West, 1989

D3. `Hey, Dumb Little Girls!' (poem)
THE DARK-HAIRED GIRL (1988)

D4. Marcus and His End (poem)
The Berkeley Gazette 21-2-44 {as by Mark Van Dyke}

D5. My Life in Stillness: White as Day (poem)
Last Wave #1, 10-83

D6. An Old Snare (poem)
A CHILD'S HAT, Gulyas, 1966

D7. On a Cat which Fell Three Stories and Survived (poem)
Last Wave #3, 1984
PKDS Newsletter (fnz) #13, 2-87

D8. Song of Philip - Five Years Old (poem) {possibly written
        by Dick's mother}
    DIVINE INVASIONS by Lawrence Sutin, Harmony, 1989
    TO THE HIGH CASTLE by Gregg Rickman, Fragments West, 1989

D9. "The Sun Was Shining Brightly" (poem)
    as part of letter to his mother, 12-May-1939
    TO THE HIGH CASTLE by Gregg Rickman, Fragments West, 1989

D10. "There Was an Old Man" (poem)
    TO THE HIGH CASTLE by Gregg Rickman, Fragments West, 1989

D11. Warning: We Are Your Police (unfilmed plot outline for
        episode of TV Drama "The Invaders")
    PKDS Newsletter (fnz) #7, 7-85
    WELCOME TO REALITY, Anton, Broken Mirrors Press, 1991

D12. Why I Am Hurt (poem)
    A CHILD'S HAT, Gulyas, 1966

E. Poem, Song, Play & TV/Film Script Volumes

E1. UBIK: THE SCREENPLAY [adapted from B61] [incl K450, K307]
    Corroboree (hb) 06-7, 6-85, 154pp, $23.00 (Valerie Hodgson;
        Int: Ron Lindahn, Val Lakey-Lindahn & Doug Rice)
        {limited to 250 copies}
    Corroboree (hb) 07-5, 6-85, 154pp, $180.00 (Valerie Hodgson;
        Int: Ron Lindahn, Val Lakey-Lindahn & Doug Rice)
        {limited to 50 leatherbound, boxed, copies, signed
        by Tim Powers & Paul Williams and with signatures
        from Dick's cheques}

F. Articles

F1. "Afterthoughts by the Author"
     THE BEST OF PHILIP K. DICK (1977)
     THE LITTLE BLACK BOX / THE EYE OF THE SIBYL (1987)
     WE CAN REMEMBER IT FOR YOU WHOLSESALE (1991) {Grafton
          edition only}

F2. "The Android and the Human"
     speech at the University of British Columbia, Vancouver,
          mid-Feb 1972
     speech at the Vancouver Science Fiction Convention,
          mid-Feb 1972
     SF Commentary (fnz) #31, 12-72
     Ashwing (fnz) #11, 1-73
     Vector (fnz) #64, 3/4-73
     PHILIP K. DICK: ELECTRIC SHEPHERD, Gillespie,
          Norstrilia, 1975
     THE DARK-HAIRED GIRL (1988)

F3. "Another Passion"
     Niekas (fnz) #28, 11-81

F4. "Breakthroughs and Breakins"
     SF Commentary (fnz) #35/36/37, 7/8/9-73

F5. "A Clarification" (letter on Stanislaw Lem)
     Science-Fiction Studies #14, 3-78
     ON PHILIP K. DICK, Mullen/Csicsery-Ronay/Evans/Hollinger,
          SF-TH Inc, 1992

F6. "The Dark-Haired Girl" (collection of letters and dreams)
     THE DARK-HAIRED GIRL (1988)

F7. "Dear Joan" (letter dated 20-May-1977)
     PKDS Newsletter (fnz) #4, 9-84
     THE SELECTED LETTERS OF PHILIP K. DICK: 1977-1979 (1993)

F8. "Dick on Dick" (selection of letters)
     New Pathways #12, 10-88

F9. "Drugs, Hallucinations, and the Quest for Reality"
     Lighthouse (fnz) #11, 11-64

F10. "The Evolution of a Vital Love"
      Mike Bailey's Personalzine (fnz) #20/21, 5-75 {as supplement}
      THE DARK-HAIRED GIRL (1988)

F11. "Fantasy" (letter to Mr. Haas, Bay Area fan, 16-Sep-1954)
      PKDS Newsletter (fnz) #29, 9-92

F12. "How to Build a Universe that Doesn't Fall Apart Two
              Days Later" (speech, probably never delivered)
      I HOPE I SHALL ARRIVE SOON (1985)

F13. "How to Write Science Fiction"
      TRANSMUTATIONS, Panshin, Elephant, 1982

F14. "If You Find This World Bad, You Should See Some of
              the Others"
      speech at the 2nd Festival International de la
              Science-Fiction de Metz, 24-Sep-1977
      L'ANNÉE 1977-1978 DE LA SCIENCE-FICTION ET DU FANTASTIQUE,
              Goimard, Juillard, 1978 {in French, as "Si Vous
              Trouvez le Monde Mauvais, Vous Devriez En Voir
              Quelques Autres"]
      PKDS Newsletter (fnz) #27, 8-91
      [staged as J19, 1991]

F15. "The Invisible" (letter to Malcolm Edwards, 6-Jun-73)
      Vector (fnz) #67/68, Spring 1974

  - "Letters from Amerika" [group title for F15, F20]

F16. "The Life of an S-F Writer" (letter to Richard Benyo,
              10-Dec-1962)
      Galactic Outpost (fnz) #2, Spring 1984 {extract, as "Tips
              for the Beginning Writer"}
      PKDS Newsletter (fnz) #26, 4-91

F17. "The Lucky Dog Pet Store" (biographical)
      Foundation #17, 9-79
      THE GOLDEN MAN (1980) {as introduction}
      PHILIP K. DICK, Greenberg/Olander, Taplinger, 1983 {as "Now
              Wait for This Year"}

F18. "Man, Android and Machine"
      SCIENCE FICTION AT LARGE, Nicholls, Gollancz, 1976;
            Fontana, 1978 (as EXPLORATIONS OF THE MARVELLOUS);
      THE DARK-HAIRED GIRL (1988)

F19. "Memories Found in a Bill from a Small Animal Vet"
      The Real World (fnz) #5, 2/3-76

F20. "Mob Rule" (letter to Malcolm Edwards, 1-Sep-1973)
      Vector (fnz) #67/68, Spring 1974

F21. "Naziism and the High Castle"
      Niekas (fnz) #9, 9-64
      PKDS Newsletter #14, 6-87

F22. "The Nixon Crowd" (letter to Bruce Gillespie, 1-Sep-1973)
      SF Commentary (fnz) #39, 11-73
      PHILIP K. DICK: ELECTRIC SHEPHERD, Gillespie,
            Norstrilia, 1975
      PKDS Newsletter (fnz) #17, 4-88
      THE SELECTED LETTERS OF PHILIP K. DICK: 1972-1973 (1993)

F23. "Notes Made Late at Night by a Weary Science Fiction Writer"
      Eternity Science Fiction #1, 7-72
      PKDS Newsletter (fnz) #22/23, 12-89

F24. "Notes (Possibly Contaminated) on an `Information Virus'"
            (letter to `Brig', 15-Apr-1981)
      PKDS Newsletter (fnz) #24, 5-90

  - "Now Wait for This Year" {see under "The Lucky Dog Pet Store"}

F25. "An Open Letter to Joanna Russ"
      Vertex 10-74

F26. "Pessimism in Science Fiction"
      Oblique (fnz) #6, 12-55
      PKDS Newsletter (fnz) #29, 9-92

F27. "PKD's Blade Runner" (1968 notes on how to film DO ANDROIDS
            DREAM OF ELECTRIC SHEEP?)
      PKDS Newsletter (fnz) #18, 8-88

F28. "Program Notes on a Great Composer"
     The Berkeley Gazette 13-9-44

F29. "A Satire on the Translating of Sixteenth Century Prophetic
          Verse"
     The Berkeley Gazette 25-1-44
     Manuscript Fall 1944

F30. "Schizophrenia & The Book of Changes"
     Niekas (fnz) #11, 3-65
     Cover (fnz) 5-74
     PKDS Newsletter (fnz) #14, 6-87

F31. "Scientists Claim: We are the Center of the Universe"
     New Worlds #216, 9-79

F32. "Self Portrait"
     PKDS Newsletter (fnz) #2, 12-83

F33. "The Short Happy Life of a Science Fiction Writer"
     Scintillation (fnz) Vol 3 #3, 6-76

F34. "The Soul of the Wub"
     FIRST VOYAGES, Knight/Greenberg/Olander, Avon, 1981
          {as Introduction to `Beyond Lies the Wub'}
     PKDS Newsletter (fnz) #24, 5-90
     Radio Free P.K.D. (fnz) #3, 10-93 {as "The Wub Lives"}

F35. "That Moon Plaque"
     MEN ON THE MOON, Wollheim, Ace, 1969 {not in 1958 edition}

F36. "Thoughts on VALIS" (excerpted from letter to John B. Ross,
          5-Mar-1979)
     New Pathways #7, 4/5-87
     THE SELECTED LETTERS OF PHILIP K. DICK: 1977-1979 (1993)

F37. "Three Sci-Fi Authors View the Future {with Michael
          Crichton & Kurt Vonnegut, Jr.}
     Voice 17-1-74

  - "Tips for the Beginning Writer" {see under "The Life of an
          S-F Writer"}

F38. "Transcript of a Seance"
     PKDS Newsletter (fnz) #12, 10-86

F39. "Universe Makers ... and Breakers"
     SelecTV Guide 15-2-81
     Radio Free P.K.D. (fnz) #1, 2-93

F40. "Was Horselover Fat a Flake?" (letters to Russell Galen,
            12-Nov-81 and 12-Jul-80)
     PKDS Newsletter (fnz) #15, 8-87

F41. "When Philip K. Dick Reviewed Himself" {Book Review of
            THE DIVINE INVASION, due for publication in
            Venom (fnz) #3 which never appeared, plus
            correspondence between Dick & Venom editors}
     The Patchin Review (fnz) #7, 1985
     PKDS Newsletter #29, 9-92 {as by Chipdip K. Kill}

F42. "Who is an SF Writer"
     SCIENCE FICTION: THE ACADEMIC AWAKENING, McNelly,
            College English Association, 1974

F43. "Will the Atomic Bomb Ever Be Perfected, and if so, What
            Becomes of Robert Heinlein"
     Lighthouse (fnz) #14, 10-66

  - "The Wub Lives" {see under "The Soul of the Wub"}

F44. "Zelazny/Varley/Gibson - and Quality"
     The New York Review of Science Fiction (fnz) #48, 8-92
            & #49, 9-92

G. Miscellaneous

G1. Afterword
    DR. ADDER by K.W. Jeter, Grafton, 1987

G2. Afterword
    DR. BLOODMONEY (1980) {Dell, Bluejay and Carroll & Graf
         editions only}

G3. Afterword
    THE GOLDEN MAN (1980)

G4. Afterword to `Faith of Our Fathers'
    DANGEROUS VISIONS, Ellison, Doubleday, 1967 {expanded in
         Signet and subsequent editions?}
    THE LITTLE BLACK BOX / THE EYE OF THE SIBYL (1987)
    WE CAN REMEMBER IT FOR YOU WHOLSESALE (1991) {Grafton
         edition only}

G5. Afterword to `A Litle Something for us Tempunauts"
    FINAL STAGE, Ferman/Malzberg, Penguin, 1975 (abridged
         version published by Charterhouse, 1974)
    THE LITTLE BLACK BOX / THE EYE OF THE SIBYL (1987)
    WE CAN REMEMBER IT FOR YOU WHOLSESALE (1991) {Grafton
         edition only}

G6. Author's Afterword to `The Days of Perky Pat'
    SF ORIGINS, Nolan/Greenberg, Popular Library, 1980
    THE DAYS OF PERKY PAT / MINORITY REPORT (1987)

G7. Author's Foreword
    A MAZE OF DEATH (1970)

G8. Author's Note
    A SCANNER DARKLY (1977)

G9. "Dick-Editors Correspondence" (letters dated 8-Nov-1951
         and 19-Mar-1952)
    THE EUREKA YEARS, McComas, Bantam, 1982

G10. Edited `The Truth' (mimeographed newspaper)
     2 issues 30-8-43, 26-10-43

G11. Excerpts from THE EXEGESIS [see H1, H3 and N6]
        The Berkeley Monthly 8-85 ("The Discovery of the True World",
            "The Information Virus", "The Black Iron Prison"
            and "Zebra Fights Back")
        Gnosis (fnz) #1, -85 ("An Excerpt")
        PKDS Newsletter (fnz) #3, 4-84 ("A Brief Excerpt from
            the Exegesis")
        PKDS Newsletter (fnz) #12, 10-86 ("An Excerpt")
        TO THE HIGH CASTLE by Gregg Rickman, Fragments West, 1989
            ("A Brief Excerpt")

G12. Four Letters to Art Spiegelman (in 1973)
        Chemical Imbalance (fnz) Vol 2 #2, 1990
        THE SELECTED LETTERS OF PHILIP K. DICK: 1972-1973 (1993)

G13. "FLOW MY TEARS - The Correspondence" (letter extracts about
            FLOW MY TEARS, THE POLICEMAN SAID)
        PKDS Newsletter (fnz) #28, 3-92

G14. Interview
        REFLECTIONS OF THE FUTURE, Hill, Ginn, 1975

G15. Interview by D. Scott Apel & Kevin C. Briggs
        PKDS Newsletter (fnz) #5, 6; 12-84, 4-85 (excerpts)
        PHILIP K. DICK: THE DREAM CONNECTION, Apel,
            Permanent Press, 1987

G16. Interview by Frank C. Bertrand
        Niekas (fnz) #36, 1988

G17. Interview by John Boonstra ("Horselover Fat and the New
            Messiah")
        The Hartford Advocate 22-4-81
        Twilight Zone 6-82 {revised and extended}
        Patchin Review (fnz) #5, 10/12-82 {pieces not used in
            Twilight Zone version}
        PKDS Newsletter (fnz) #1, 8-83 {excerpt}
        [released on tape as J11, 1991]
        PKDS Newsletter (fnz) #29, 9-92 {excerpt as "Comments on
            CONFESSIONS OF A CRAP ARTIST"}

G18. Interview by George Cain & Dana Longo ("Philip K. Dick:
            Confessions of a SF Artist")
        Denver Clarion 23-10-80

G19. Interview by Arthur Byron Cover
        Vertex 2-74

G20. Interview by Patrice Davis ("Rencontre avec Philip K. Dick")
        Galaxie #100, 9-72 {in French}

G21. Interview by Daniel DePrez
        Science Fiction Review (fnz) #19, 8-76

G22. Interview by Mike Hodel ("The Mainstream that through the
                Ghetto Flows")
        Pacifica Radio, Los Angeles, 13-6-76
        Missouri Review Vol VII #2, 1984

G23. Interview by Gwen Lee & Doris E. Sauter
        Starlog #150, 1-90 (part 1) ("Thinker of Antiquity")
        Starlog #165, 4-91 (part 2) ("Worlds of Sound and Colour")

G24. Interview by Richard A. Lupoff ("A Conversation with Philip
                K. Dick")
        broadcast on KPFA FM Berkeley, 11-77
        Science Fiction Eye (fnz) #2, 8-87

G25. Interview by Gary & Nicole Panter
        Slash (fnz) Vol 3 #5, 5-80

G26. Interview/Profile by Charles Platt ("Reality in Drag")
        Ad Astra #9, 3-80 {slightly revised as "The Ideos Cosmos
                of Philip K. Dick"}
        Science Fiction Review (fnz) #36, 8-80
        WHO WRITES SCIENCE FICTION, Platt, Savoy, 1980; Berkley (as
                THE DREAM MAKERS); Xanadu, 1987 (contents differ,
                as THE DREAM MAKERS);

G27. Interview by Philip Purser
        London Daily Telegraph 12-73

G28. Interview by Gregg Rickman ("Philip K. Dick's Last Interview")
        Uncle Jam International (fnz) 5-82
        PHILIP K. DICK: THE LAST TESTAMENT by Gregg Rickman,
                Fragments West, 1985

G29. Interview by Gregg Rickman ("Piper in the Woods: Philip K.
          Dick on Life and Death")
     [recorded as J23]
     Argosy 11-90 {excerpt}

G30. Interview by James van Hise ("Philip K. Dick on Bladerunner")
     Starlog #55, 2-82

G31. Interview by Joe Vitale ("The Worlds of Philip K. Dick")
     The Aquarian 11-10-78

G32. Interview by Paul Williams ("The True Stories of
          Philip K. Dick")
     Rolling Stone #199, 6-11-75
     ONLY APPARENTLY REAL, Williams, Arbor House, 1986 {expanded}

G33. "Introducing the Author" (with photo)
     Imagination 2-53
     TO THE HIGH CASTLE by Gregg Rickman, Fragments West, 1989

G34. Introduction to `The Android and the Human'
     PHILIP K. DICK: ELECTRIC SHEPHERD, Gillespie,
          Norstrilia, 1975

G35. Introduction to THE PRESERVING MACHINE (unpublished as such)
     Science-Fiction Studies #5, 3-75
     BEYOND LIES THE WUB / THE SHORT HAPPY LIFE OF THE BROWN
          OXFORD (1987) {extract}
     ON PHILIP K. DICK, Mullen/Csicsery-Ronay/Evans/Hollinger,
          SF-TH Inc, 1992

G36. Introduction to `Roog'
     Unearth Winter 1979
     BEYOND LIES THE WUB / THE SHORT HAPPY LIFE OF THE BROWN
          OXFORD (1987)

G37. "A Letter from Philip K. Dick, February 1, 1960" (to Eleanor
          Dimoff at Harcourt, Brace & World concerning
          mainstream novels)
     PKDS Pamphlet (fnz) #1, 8-83

G38. Letter (written 1981)
     The Missouri Review Vol VII #2, 1984

G39. Letter
     Niekas (fnz) #26, 5-81

G40. Letter
     Niekas (fnz) #29, 2-82

G41. Letter
     Rolling Stone 12-12-75

G42. Letter (on Berlin Uprising of 1953) ("The Spirit of '53")
     San Francisco Chronicle 7-7-53

G43. Letter
     Scintillation (fnz) #12, 3-77

G44. Letter (on Herman Wouk)
     Time 3-10-55

G45. Letter
     Vector (fnz) #65, 5/6-73

G46. Letter to Scott Apel, 8-8-80
     PHILIP K. DICK: THE DREAM CONNECTION, Apel,
          Permanent Press, 1987

G47. "A Letter to Anthony Boucher"
     PKDS Newsletter #30, 12-92

G48. Letter to Anthony Boucher, 26-May-1964
     Radio Free P.K.D. (fnz) #2, 5-93

G49. Letter to Joe and Laura, 9-Jul-1981
     THE DARK-HAIRED GIRL (1988)

G50. Letter to John Betancourt, 14-May-1981
     BEYOND LIES THE WUB / THE SHORT HAPPY LIFE OF THE BROWN
          OXFORD (1987) {extract}

G51. Letter to Edgar Dick, 8-Sep-1973
     THE DARK-HAIRED GIRL (1988)
     THE SELECTED LETTERS OF PHILIP K. DICK: 1972-1973 (1993)

G52. Letter to Edgar Dick, 9-Sep-1973
    THE DARK-HAIRED GIRL (1988)
    THE SELECTED LETTERS OF PHILIP K. DICK: 1972-1973 (1993)

G53. Letter to Richard Geis, 7-Jun-1973
    The Alien Critic (fnz) #6, 8-73
    THE SELECTED LETTERS OF PHILIP K. DICK: 1972-1973 (1993)

G54. Letter to Richard Geis
    Science Fiction Review (fnz) #39, Summer 1981

G55. Letter to Bruce Gillespie, 8-Jun-1969
    SF Commentary (fnz) #9, 2-70
    PHILIP K. DICK: ELECTRIC SHEPHERD, Gillespie,
        Norstrilia, 1975

G56. Letter to Bruce Gillespie, 9-Sep-1970
    SF Commentary (fnz) #17, 11-70
    PKD: A PHILIP K. DICK BIBLIOGRAPHY by Daniel J.H. Levack
        & Steven Owen Godersky, Underwood-Miller, 1981
        {as Afterword}

G57. Letter to David Hartwell, 21-May-1981 (containing outline
        for THE OWL IN DAYLIGHT)
    Forced Exposure (fnz) #13, Winter 1988
    PHILIP K. DICK: A CELEBRATION, Merrifield/Joyce,
        Connections, 1991

G58. Letter to Mr. Hollis, 16-Dec-1949
    PKDS Newsletter (fnz) #11, 5-86

G59. Letter to Robert Jaffe, 4-Mar-1975 (on the film of UBIK)
    PKDS Newsletter (fnz) #11, 5-86 {extract}
    THE SELECTED LETTERS OF PHILIP K. DICK: 1975-1976 (1992)

G60. Letter to Scott Meredith, 2-Aug-1970
    PKDS Newsletter (fnz) #12, 10-86

G61. Letter to Jack Scovil, 3-Mar-1975 (on the film of UBIK)
    PKDS Newsletter (fnz) #11, 5-86 {extract}
    THE SELECTED LETTERS OF PHILIP K. DICK: 1975-1976 (1992)

G62. Letter to Susan Sontag, 28-Feb-1975 (on the film of UBIK)
       PKDS Newsletter (fnz) #11, 5-86
       THE SELECTED LETTERS OF PHILIP K. DICK: 1975-1976 (1992)

G63. Letter to Patricia S. Warrick, 11-Sep-1978
       PHILIP K. DICK: THE DREAM CONNECTION, Apel,
              Permanent Press, 1987
       THE SELECTED LETTERS OF PHILIP K. DICK: 1977-1979 (1993)

G64. Memoir (Notes on `The Golden Man')
       WORLDS OF IF: A RETROSPECTIVE ANTHOLOGY,
              Pohl/Greenberg/Olander, Bluejay, 1986
       THE FATHER-THING (1987)
       SECOND VARIETY (1991) {Citadel Twilight edition only}

G65. Memoir (Notes on `Oh, to be a Blobel')
       GALAXY: THIRTY YEARS OF INNOVATIVE SCIENCE FICTION,
              Pohl/Olander/Greenberg, Playboy, 1980
       THE DAYS OF PERKY PAT / THE MINORITY REPORT (1987)

G66. Part of Guest Editorial on Anthony Boucher
       Fantasy and Science Fiction 8-68

G67. Predictions
       THE BOOK OF PREDICTIONS, Wallechinsky, Morrow, 1981

G68. Prescript to FLOW MY TEARS, THE POLICEMAN SAID
       PKDS Newsletter (fnz) #12, 10-86

G69. Prologue to EYE IN THE SKY
       PKDS Newsletter (fnz) #13, 2-87

G70. Response to Questionnaire
       THE DOUBLE:BILL SYMPOSIUM, Bowers/Mallardi, D:B Press, 1969

G71. The "Tagore" Letter
       PHILIP K. DICK: THE DREAM CONNECTION, Apel,
              Permanent Press, 1987
       PHILIP K. DICK: THE LAST TESTAMENT by Gregg Rickman,
              Fragments West, 1985

G72. Unique Sinister Type Notification {with Jack Newton}
       Niekas (fnz) #10, 12-64

G73. Story Notes
In addition, Dick wrote a number of story notes for
THE GOLDEN MAN and THE BEST OF PHILIP K. DICK. They were
all reprinted in PKD: A BIBLIOGRAPHY and have otherwise
appeared as follows:

Autofac
  THE BEST OF PHILIP K. DICK (1977)
  THE DAYS OF PERKY PAT / THE MINORITY REPORT (1987)

Beyond Lies the Wub
  THE BEST OF PHILIP K. DICK (1977)
  BEYOND LIES THE WUB / THE SHORT HAPPY LIFE OF THE BROWN
      OXFORD (1987)

Breakfast at Twilight
  THE BEST OF PHILIP K. DICK (1977)
  SECOND VARIETY (1987) {not in Citadel Twilight edition}
  WE CAN REMEMBER IT FOR YOU WHOLESALE (1990)
      {Citadel Twilight edition only}

Colony
  THE BEST OF PHILIP K. DICK (1977)
  BEYOND LIES THE WUB / THE SHORT HAPPY LIFE OF THE BROWN
      OXFORD (1987)

The Days of Perky Pat [see also G6]
  THE BEST OF PHILIP K. DICK (1977)
  THE DAYS OF PERKY PAT / THE MINORITY REPORT (1987)

The Electric Ant
  THE BEST OF PHILIP K. DICK (1977)
  THE LITTLE BLACK BOX / THE EYE OF THE SIBYL (1987)
  WE CAN REMEMBER IT FOR YOU WHOLSESALE (1991) {Grafton
      edition only}

Expendable
  THE BEST OF PHILIP K. DICK (1977)
  BEYOND LIES THE WUB / THE SHORT HAPPY LIFE OF THE BROWN
      OXFORD (1987)

Faith of Our Fathers
  THE BEST OF PHILIP K. DICK (1977)
  THE LITTLE BLACK BOX / THE EYE OF THE SIBYL (1987)
  WE CAN REMEMBER IT FOR YOU WHOLSESALE (1991) {Grafton
      edition only}

The Father-Thing
  THE BEST OF PHILIP K. DICK (1977)
  THE FATHER-THING (1987)
  SECOND VARIETY (1991) {Citadel Twilight edition only}

G73. Story Notes (cont)
     Foster, You're Dead!
       THE BEST OF PHILIP K. DICK (1977)
       THE FATHER-THING (1987)
       SECOND VARIETY (1991) {Citadel Twilight edition only}

     A Game of Unchance
       THE GOLDEN MAN (1980)
       THE LITTLE BLACK BOX / THE EYE OF THE SIBYL (1987)
       WE CAN REMEMBER IT FOR YOU WHOLSESALE (1991) {Grafton
            edition only}

     The Golden Man [see also G64]
       THE GOLDEN MAN (1980)
       THE FATHER-THING (1987)
       SECOND VARIETY (1991) {Citadel Twilight edition only}

     Human Is
       THE BEST OF PHILIP K. DICK (1977)
       SECOND VARIETY (1987) {not in Citadel Twilight edition}
       WE CAN REMEMBER IT FOR YOU WHOLESALE (1990)
            {Citadel Twilight edition only}

     If There Were No Benny Cemoli
       THE BEST OF PHILIP K. DICK (1977)
       THE DAYS OF PERKY PAT / THE MINORITY REPORT (1987)

     Impostor
       THE BEST OF PHILIP K. DICK (1977)
       SECOND VARIETY (1987) {not in Citadel Twilight edition}
       WE CAN REMEMBER IT FOR YOU WHOLESALE (1990)
            {Citadel Twilight edition only}

     The King of the Elves
       THE GOLDEN MAN (1980)
       BEYOND LIES THE WUB / THE SHORT HAPPY LIFE OF THE BROWN
            OXFORD (1987)

     The Last of the Masters
       THE GOLDEN MAN (1980)
       THE FATHER-THING (1987)
       SECOND VARIETY (1991) {Citadel Twilight edition only}

     The Little Black Box
       THE GOLDEN MAN (1980)
       THE LITTLE BLACK BOX / THE EYE OF THE SIBYL (1987)
       WE CAN REMEMBER IT FOR YOU WHOLSESALE (1991) {Grafton
            edition only}

     A Little Something for Us Tempunauts
       THE BEST OF PHILIP K. DICK (1977)
       THE LITTLE BLACK BOX / THE EYE OF THE SIBYL (1987)
       WE CAN REMEMBER IT FOR YOU WHOLSESALE (1991) {Grafton
            edition only}

G73. Story Notes (cont)
     Meddler
          THE GOLDEN MAN (1980)
          BEYOND LIES THE WUB / THE SHORT HAPPY LIFE OF THE BROWN
               OXFORD (1987)

     The Mold of Yancy
          THE GOLDEN MAN (1980)
          THE DAYS OF PERKY PAT / THE MINORITY REPORT (1987)

     Not By Its Cover
          THE GOLDEN MAN (1980)
          THE LITTLE BLACK BOX / THE EYE OF THE SIBYL (1987)
          WE CAN REMEMBER IT FOR YOU WHOLSESALE (1991) {Grafton
               edition only}

     Oh, To Be A Blobel! [see also G65]
          THE BEST OF PHILIP K. DICK (1977)
          THE DAYS OF PERKY PAT / THE MINORITY REPORT (1987)

     Paycheck
          THE BEST OF PHILIP K. DICK (1977)
          BEYOND LIES THE WUB / THE SHORT HAPPY LIFE OF THE BROWN
               OXFORD (1987)

     Precious Artifact
          THE GOLDEN MAN (1980)
          THE LITTLE BLACK BOX / THE EYE OF THE SIBYL (1987)
          WE CAN REMEMBER IT FOR YOU WHOLSESALE (1991) {Grafton
               edition only}

     The Pre-Persons
          THE GOLDEN MAN (1980)
          THE LITTLE BLACK BOX / THE EYE OF THE SIBYL (1987)
          WE CAN REMEMBER IT FOR YOU WHOLSESALE (1991) {Grafton
               edition only}

     Return Match
          THE GOLDEN MAN (1980)
          THE LITTLE BLACK BOX / THE EYE OF THE SIBYL (1987)
          WE CAN REMEMBER IT FOR YOU WHOLSESALE (1991) {Grafton
               edition only}

     Roog [see also G36]
          THE BEST OF PHILIP K. DICK (1977)
          BEYOND LIES THE WUB / THE SHORT HAPPY LIFE OF THE BROWN
               OXFORD (1987)

     Sales Pitch
          THE GOLDEN MAN (1980)
          THE FATHER-THING (1987)
          SECOND VARIETY (1991) {Citadel Twilight edition only}

G73. Story Notes (cont)
    Second Variety
        THE BEST OF PHILIP K. DICK (1977)
        SECOND VARIETY (1987)

    Service Call
        THE BEST OF PHILIP K. DICK (1977)
        THE DAYS OF PERKY PAT / THE MINORITY REPORT (1987)

    Small Town
        THE GOLDEN MAN (1980)
        SECOND VARIETY (1987) {not in Citadel Twilight edition}
        WE CAN REMEMBER IT FOR YOU WHOLESALE (1990)
            {Citadel Twilight edition only}

    The Unreconstructed M
        THE GOLDEN MAN (1980)
        THE DAYS OF PERKY PAT / THE MINORITY REPORT (1987)

    The War with the Fnools
        THE GOLDEN MAN (1980)
        THE LITTLE BLACK BOX / THE EYE OF THE SIBYL (1987)
        WE CAN REMEMBER IT FOR YOU WHOLSESALE (1991) {Grafton
            edition only}

H. *Non-Fiction Books*

H1. COSMOGONY AND COSMOLOGY [incl K441]
    Kerosina (hb) 17-6, 11-87, 45pp {limited to 325 copies
        distributed with the collector's edition of VALIS}
    Kerosina (tp) 18-4, 11-87, 45pp, £4.50 (Keith Roberts)
        {limited to 500 copies}

H2. THE DARK-HAIRED GIRL [C-9: K442, F6, F2, D3, F10, G51,
        G52, F18, G49, A44]
    Zeising (hb) 03-1, 12-88, 246pp, $19.95 (Mark Bilokur)
        {limited to 4000 copies}

H3. IN PURSUIT OF VALIS: SELECTIONS FROM THE EXEGESIS [incl K386,
        K220, K456, K267] {edited by Lawrence Sutin}
    Underwood-Miller (hb) 091-6, 11-91, 278pp, $39.95 (Ilene Meyer)
    Underwood-Miller (hb) 092-4, 11-91, 278pp, $75.00 (Meyer)
        {limited to 250 numbered, slipcased, copies,
        signed by Lawrence Sutin}
    Underwood-Miller (tp) 093-2, 11-91, 278pp, $14.95 (Meyer)

H4. THE SELECTED LETTERS OF PHILIP K. DICK: 1972-1973
           [incl K135, F22, G51, G52, G53, G12]
      Underwood-Miller (hb) 161-0, 10-93, 387pp, $39.95 (Ilene Meyer)
      Underwood-Miller (hb) 162-9, 10-93, 387pp, $60.00 (Meyer)
           {limited to 250 numbered, slipcased, copies,
           signed by Dennis Etchison}

H5. THE SELECTED LETTERS OF PHILIP K. DICK: 1974 [incl K165,
           K438, K247, K149]
      Underwood-Miller (hb) 104-1, 5-91, 314pp, $39.95 (Ilene Meyer)
           {limited to 625 copies}; -91 {600 copies};
      Underwood-Miller (hb) 105-X, 5-91, 314pp, $60.00 (Meyer)
           {limited to 250 numbered, slipcased, copies signed
           by William Gibson}
      Underwood-Miller (hb)   , 5-91, 314pp, $200.00 (Meyer)
           {limited to 26 lettered, slipcased, copies signed
           by William Gibson and with a Dick signature tipped in}

H6. THE SELECTED LETTERS OF PHILIP K. DICK: 1975-1976 [incl K310,
           G59, G61, G62] {edited by Don Herron}
      Underwood-Miller (hb) 111-4, 12-92, 351pp, $39.95 (Ilene Meyer)
      Underwood-Miller (hb) 112-2, 12-92, 351pp, $60.00 (Meyer)
           {limited to 250 numbered, slipcased, copies signed
           by Tim Powers}

H7. THE SELECTED LETTERS OF PHILIP K. DICK: 1977-1979 [incl K462,
           G63, F7, F36] {edited by Don Herron}
      Underwood-Miller (hb) 120-3, 7-93, 260pp, $39.95 (Ilene Meyer)
      Underwood-Miller (hb) 121-1, 7-93, 260pp, $60.00 (Meyer)
           {limited to 250 numbered, slipcased, copies signed
           by Robert Anton Wilson}

I. Edited Books

      None Known

J. Other Media

      J1. BLADE RUNNER [based on B18]
           Film starring Harrison Ford & Rutger Hauer, directed by
           Ridley Scott, 1982

      J2. The Religious Experience of Philip K. Dick by Robert Crumb
               (cartoon version of the Valis visions)
           Weirdo #17, 1986

J3. Claw [A110]
   Unfinished Screenplay by Dan O'Bannon

J4. Colony (radio play) [A16]
   X Minus One 10-10-56
   Moonlight Productions MP1008C, -80, £4.95 (cassette, with
       "How To" by Clifford D. Simak)

J5. CONFESSIONS D'UN BARJO [B9]
   French film directed by Jerome Boivin, and starring Richard
   Bohringer, Hyppolite Girardot & Anne Brochet, 5-92.

J6. The Cookie Lady [A18]
   TV presentation aired on Metromedia, some time in
   the 1970s.

J7. The Defenders (radio play) [A24]
   X Minus One 22-May-1956
   Issued on cassette in 1961 by Living Literature, Inc.
   Moonlight Productions MP1002C, -80, £4.95 (cassette, with
       "A Pail of Air" by Fritz Leiber}

J8. The Father Thing [A37]
   Stage production by The Youth Theatre, directed by Denise
   Rose, at Philip K. Dick: A Celebration, Epping Forest
   College, 19/20-Oct-1991.

J9. Final Defence (radio script)
   Exploring Tomorrow, WOR, 1958

J10. FLOW MY TEARS, THE POLICEMAN SAID [B23]
   Stage adaptation by Linda Hartinian, performed by Mabou
   Mines, at the Boston Shakespeare 18-6-85 to 30-6-85.
   Script published in 1991 by The Dramatic Publishing Company
   of Woodstock (57pp, $4.75).

J11. Horselover Fat and the New Messiah [G17]
   110-minute interview by John Boonstra, available on cassette
   tape for $16.49, 1991.

J12. Human Is [A52]
   Stage production by The Youth Theatre, directed by Keaton
   O'Rourke, at Philip K. Dick: A Celebration, Epping Forest
   College, 19/20-Oct-1991.

J13. Impostor [A56]
     Out of this World 21-7-62, adapted by Terry Nation and
     Starring John Carson and Patrick Allen.

J14. Impostor (radio script) [A56]
     Sci-Fi Radio (Public Radio) 1989

J15. Made in Avack (radio play) [adapted as A141]
     Exploring Tomorrow, WOR, 1957-58

J16. The Man Who Fell (radio script) [A104] {also known as
               Dreams}
     Exploring Tomorrow, WOR, 2-58

J17. MARTIAN TIME-SLIP [B38]
     Televised by the BBC in the 1960s

J18. MARTIAN TIME-SLIP [B38]
     Stage adaptation by Joel Gersmann, performed at the Broom
     Street Theater, Madison, Wisconsin on 18-Sep-1987.

J19. The Metz Speech [F14]
     Staged and performed by John Dowie at Philip K. Dick: A
     Celebration, Epping Forest College, 19/20-Oct-1991.

J20. New Economic Fact (radio script)
     Exploring Tomorrow, WOR, 2-58 (possibly not broadcast)

J21. NINETY MINUTES WITH PHILIP K. DICK (excerpts from an
               extended interview with Dick and Dick's own
               audio notes on a novel in progres)
     Audiocassette issued as PKDS Newsletter (fnz) #9/10, 1-86

J22. Philip K. Dick: A Day in the Afterlife
     BBC Documentary on Dick, broadcast on BBC2, 9th April 1994,
     7:35PM - 8:35PM in the "Arena" series [discussed in K242]

J23. Piper in the Woods [G29]
     Fragments West   , $10.00

J24. RADIO FREE ALBEMUTH [B51]
     Adapted as a two-act play by Lisa Morton, Theatre of
     N.O.T.E, Hollywood. Performed 22, 23, 29, 30-Jan-1991,
     5, 6, 12, 13, 19, 20, 26, 27-Feb-1991.

J25. Sales Pitch [A108]
     Adapted by Brad Schreiber for Sci-Fi Radio (Public Radio) 1989

J26. The Short Happy Life of the Brown Oxford [A113]
     Read by Ed Begley, Jr. on "Literary Evenings at the Met",
     13-Mar-1993.

J27. Take Them to the Garden (Play constructed from assorted
                PKD essays, interviews, story notes & such-like;
                directed by John Dowie, starring John Joyce)
     Performed at Finborough Theatre Club, London, 18-Oct-1989
     Performed at Edinburgh Festival 1990
     Performed at Philip K. Dick: A Celebration, Epping Forest
            College, 19/20-Oct-1991.
     U Productions (ph) , -90, 18pp, 50p
            {limited to 500 copies}

J28. TOTAL RECALL [based on A145]
     Film starring Arnold Schwarzenegger, Michael Ironside and
     Sharon Stone, directed by Paul Verhoeven, 1990.

J29. THE TRANSMIGRATION OF TIMOTHY ARCHER [B60]
     Stage adaptation by Geoff Ryman, first performed at
     Tynecon II, 27-May-1984.

J30. VALIS (an opera by Tod Machover) [based on B63]
     Bridge Records   , -88, $10.98 (cassette) or $18.98 (CD)
     Performed at The Cube, MIT, Cambridge, Massachusetts on
            16-6-89 and 17-6-89.

J31. What is Human
     Play based on PKD's writings & performed by John Joyce
     at Philip K. Dick: A Celebration, Epping Forest
     College, 19/20-Oct-1991.

K. Articles on Philip K. Dick

K1. Article on Martin Amis, TIME'S ARROW and Dick
    Evening Standard 5-11-81

K2. Article/Review Column on Dick
    The New Republic 6-12-93

K3. Bibliography
    Portti 7-93 {in Finnish}

K4. Biographical Sketch
    Fantastic 9/10-53
    New Worlds #89, 12-59 (+ photo)
    SF Monthly (Aust) #12, 8-56
    THE DIVINE INVASION (1982) {Corgi edition}
    TIME OUT OF JOINT (1976) {Penguin edition}
    THE TRANSMIGRATION OF TIMOTHY ARCHER (1983) {Timescape
           edition}
    WE CAN BUILD YOU (1972) {DAW edition}
    FINAL STAGE, Ferman/Malzberg, Penguin, 1975

K5. Entry
    WHO'S WHO IN AMERICA 1981-1982
    PKDS Newsletter (fnz) #3, 4-84

K6. Obituary
    Asahi Evening News

K7. Obituary
    San Francisco Chronicle 3-3-82 (?)

K8. "Arbor House to issue Last Philip K. Dick Novel"
    Publishers Weekly 31-5-85

K9. "Court Petitioned in Phil Dick Estate"
    Locus (fnz) #270, 7-83

K10. "Les Delires Vrais de Philip K. Dick"
     Le Nouvel Observateur 24/30-6-93 {in French}

K11. "Do Androids Dream of Philip K. Dick?"
     Portti 7-93 {in Finnish}

K12. "Editors' Letters to Philip K. Dick: 1955-1959"
     PKDS Newsletter (fnz) #17, 4-88

K13. "Editors' Letters to Philip K. Dick: 1960"
     PKDS Newsletter (fnz) #24, 5-90

K14. "In the Afternoon, We Drove Over to Fullerton to See
             Philip K. Dick"
     The New Yorker 3-2-75

K15. "Most Prolific Dead Author?"
     Locus (fnz) #287, 12-84

K16. "Other Authors, Other Worlds"
     The Economist #301, 1986

K17. "Philip Dick (Update)"
     BEACHAM'S POPULAR FICTION 1991 UPDATE, Beacham, Beacham, 1991

K18. "Philip K. Dick (Obituary)"
     SFWA Bulletin 5-82

K19. "Philip K. Dick, dead, is now larger than life"
     Science Fiction Chronicle (fnz) 12-84

K20. "Philip K. Dick Movie Nears Completion"
     Locus (fnz) #254, 3-82

K21. "Philip K. Dick: 1928 - 1982"
     Science Fiction Chronicle (fnz) 5-82

K22. "Philip K. Dick suffers Stroke, in Coma, Critical Condition;
             Dies"
     Science Fiction Chronicle (fnz) 4-82

K23. "Philip K. Dick Weekend"
     Locus (fnz) #372, 1-92

K24. "Philip K. Dick, won Awards for Science-Fiction Works"
     New York Times 3-3-82

K25. "P.K. Dick's FLOW MY TEARS... to be Performed in NYC"
     Science Fiction Chronicle (fnz) 6-88

K26. "Schizophrenia, The I Ching & Philip K. Dick" [assorted
           comments on F30]
     Niekas (fnz) #12, 6-65

K27. "Science Fiction Author Philip K. Dick Dies"
     Fullerton Daily News Tribune 3-3-82

K28. "Sci-Fi's Philip Dick Dies"
     Fullerton Register 3-3-82

K29. "Some Thoughts on Philip K. Dick"
     Science Fiction Chronicle (fnz) 5-82

K30. "Three Sci-Fi Authors View the Future"
     Scholastic Voice 17-1-74

K31. "The Transmigration of Philip K. Dick"
     Locus (fnz) #273, 10-83

K32. "Vintage Philip K. Dick"
     Locus (fnz) #355, 8-90

K33. "Walk of the Town"
     Oakland Tribune 10-1-55
     PKDS Newsletter (fnz) #2, 12-83

K34. "Elusive Utopias: Societies as Mechanisms in the Early
           Fiction of Philip K. Dick" by Merritt Abrash
     CLOCKWORK WORLDS, Erlich, Greenwood, 1983

K35. "A Failure of Scholarship" by Merritt Abrash [review of
           THE NOVELS OF PHILIP K. DICK by Kim Stanley Robinson]
     Science Fiction Studies #37, 11-85 (Merritt Abrash)
     ON PHILIP K. DICK, Mullen/Csicsery-Ronay/Evans/Hollinger,
           SF-TH Inc, 1992

K36. "In Response to George Slusser" by Merritt Abrash [letter
            on K357]
        Science Fiction Studies #42, 7-87
        ON PHILIP K. DICK, Mullen/Csicsery-Ronay/Evans/Hollinger,
            SF-TH Inc, 1992

K37. "`Man Everywhere in Chains: Dick', Rousseau, and THE
            PENULTIMATE TRUTH" by Merritt Abrash
        Foundation #39, Spring 1987

K38. "Sparring with the Universe: Heroism and Futility in
            Philip K. Dick's Universe" by Merritt Abrash
        Extrapolation Vol 27 #2, Summer 1986

K39. "Two Forms of Metafantasy" by George Aichele, Jr.
        Journal of the Fantastic in the Arts Vol 1 #3, 1988

K40. "Mystery Still Surrounds Death of Local Sci-Fi Author"
            by David Alcott
        The Tribune (Oakland) 28-8-83

K41. "Dick's Maledictory Web: About and Around MARTIAN TIME-SLIP"
            by Brian W. Aldiss
        Science-Fiction Studies #5, 3-75
        MARTIAN TIME-SLIP (1976) {NEL editions, as introduction}
        THIS WORLD AND NEARER ONES by Brian W. Aldiss,
            Weidenfeld & Nicolson, 1979
        PHILIP K. DICK, Greenberg/Olander, Taplinger, 1983
        ON PHILIP K. DICK, Mullen/Csicsery-Ronay/Evans/Hollinger,
            SF-TH Inc, 1992

K42. "Philip K. Dick Appreciation" by Brian W. Aldiss
        Locus (fnz) #256, 5-82

K43. "Philip K. Dick: A Whole New Can of Worms" by Brian W. Aldiss
        Talk at the City Literary Institute, London, 9-6-82
        Foundation #26, 10-82
        THE PALE SHADOW OF SCIENCE by Brian W. Aldiss, Serconia, 1985

K44. "Motherness Creations: Motifs in Science Fiction" by John
            Allman
        North Dakota Quarterly Spring 1990

K45. "Philip K. Dick Appreciation" by Poul Anderson
Locus (fnz) #256, 5-82

K46. "The Half-Life of Philip K. Dick" by Uwe Anton
WELCOME TO REALITY, Anton, Broken Mirrors Press, 1991
{translated by Jim Young} {as Introduction}

K47. Obituary by Steven Anzovin
THE ANNUAL OBITUARY 1982, Bodell, St. James Press, 1983

K48. Preface by D. Scott Apel
PHILIP K. DICK: THE DREAM CONNECTION, Apel,
Permanent Press, 1987

K49. "Phil as I Knew Him" by D. Scott Apel
PHILIP K. DICK: THE DREAM CONNECTION, Apel,
Permanent Press, 1987 {as introduction}

K50. "Philip K. Dick: The Dream Connection" by D. Scott Apel
PHILIP K. DICK: THE DREAM CONNECTION, Apel,
Permanent Press, 1987

K51. Entry by Brian Ash
WHO'S WHO IN SCIENCE FICTION by Brian Ash, Taplinger, 1976

K52. Checklist of Author's Works April 1956 - March 1966 by
Michael Ashley
THE HISTORY OF THE SCIENCE FICTION MAGAZINE: PART 4:
1956-1965, Ashley, NEL, 1978

K53. "Cult Classic Sci-Fi Novelist: Philip K. Dick" by Mike Ashley
Book and Magazine Collector #74, 5-90

K54. "MARTIAN TIME-SLIP" by Richard Astle
SURVEY OF SCIENCE FICTION LITERATURE VOL 3, Magill,
Salem Press, 1979

K55. "Reality, Religion, and Politics in Philip K. Dick's Fiction"
by Aaron John Barlow
Dissertation Abstracts International #49, 2-89

K56. "The Morigny Conference" by Jean-Pierre Barricelli
Science-Fiction Studies #45, 7-88 {as afterword}
ON PHILIP K. DICK, Mullen/Csicsery-Ronay/Evans/Hollinger,
SF-TH Inc, 1992

K57. "Madman's Ravings or Relevant Message?" by Lewis Beale
Atlanta Journal & Constitution 18-8-91

K58. "Philip Dick: When Sci-Fi Becomes Real" by Lewis Beale
Philadelphia Inquirer 7-91
Detroit Free Press
New York Newsday
Los Angeles Times 8-8-91
Newsbank. Literature 75, 1991

K59. "In Philip K. Dick Territory" by Rick Bennett
PKDS Newsletter (fnz) #3, 4-84

K60. "God's New Age Prophet" by Mark Berman & David Newnham
The Guardian 24-7-90

K61. "The Electric Dreams of Philip K. Dick" by Richard Bernstein
New York Times Book Review 3-11-91

K62. "Encounters with Reality: P.K. Dick's A SCANNER DARKLY" by
F.C. Bertrand
Philosophical Speculations in SF and Fantasy 3-81

K63. "Kant's `Noumenal Self' and Doppelganger in P.K. Dick's
A SCANNER DARKLY" by F.C. Bertrand
Philosophical Speculations in SF and Fantasy Summer 1981

K64. "In Pursuit of UBIK" by Michael Bishop
UBIK (1979) {Gregg Press edition only}
Starship (fnz) Summer 1980
PHILIP K. DICK, Greenberg/Olander, Taplinger, 1983

K65. "Blade Runner Revisited" by D.S. Black
PKDS Newsletter (fnz) #28, 3-92

K66. "Puttering About the Silver Screen: The Story of UBIK: The
Movie" by D.S. Black
PKDS Newsletter (fnz) #11, 5-86

K67. Article by James P. Blaylock
Firsts 10-94

K68. Introduction by James P. Blaylock
THE BROKEN BUBBLE (1988) {Ultramarine edition only}

K69. "The Phil Wars" by James P. Blaylock, K.W. Jeter & Tim Powers
Panel at Armadillocon 10, 10-88
PKDS Newsletter (fnz) #20, 4-89

K70. "Paperback Originals of Philip K. Dick" by D.Z. Block
Paperback Quarterly Fall 1982

K71. Article by John Boonstra
Hartford Advocate 31-10-84

K72. "VALIS - The Opera" by Keith Bowden
PKDS Newsletter (fnz) #17, 4-88

K73. "Dick in France: A Love Story" by Roger Bozzetto
Science-Fiction Studies #45, 7-88 {translated by Danièle
Chatelain & George Slusser}
ON PHILIP K. DICK, Mullen/Csicsery-Ronay/Evans/Hollinger,
SF-TH Inc, 1992 {translated by Danièle
Chatelain & George Slusser}

K74. "Mandalic Activism: An Approach to Structure, Theme and Tone
in Four Novels by Philip K. Dick" by Mary K. Bray
Extrapolation Summer 1980

K75. "Walking in an Agoraphobe's Wonderland" by Dwight Brown
GATHER YOURSELVES TOGETHER (1994) {as Afterword}

K76. "Philip K. Dick Dies" by Charles N. Brown
Locus (fnz) #255, 4-82

K77. "The Two Tractates of Philip K. Dick" by Steve Brown
Science Fiction Review (fnz) #39, 2-81

K78. Introduction by John Brunner
THE FATHER-THING (1987)
SECOND VARIETY (1991) {Citadel Twilight edition only}

K79. "Philip K. Dick Appreciation" by John Brunner
Locus (fnz) #256, 5-82

K80. "The Reality of Philip K. Dick" by John Brunner
THE BEST OF PHILIP K. DICK (1977)

K81. "The Work of Philip K. Dick" by John Brunner
New Worlds #166, 9-66

K82. "Ramble City: Postmodernism and BLADE RUNNER" by Giulana Bruno
October #41, Summer 1987
ALIEN ZONE, Kuhn, Verso, 1990

K83. "PKD" by Vic Bullock
Blade Runner Souvenir Magazine #1, 1982

K84. "Philip K. Dick and the Metaphysics of American Politics" by
Brian J. Burden
Foundation #26, 10-82

K85. Letter by Andrew M. Butler [on K172]
Critical Wave (fnz) #23, 1991

K86. "Reality Versus Transience: An Examination of Philip K.
Dick's DO ANDROIDS DREAM OF ELECTRIC SHEEP? and
Ridley Scott's BLADE RUNNER" by Andrew M. Butler
PHILIP K. DICK: A CELEBRATION, Merrifield/Joyce,
Connections, 1991

K87. "Commodity Futures: Corporate State and Personal Style in
Three Recent Science-Fiction Movies" by
Thomas B. Byers
Science Fiction Studies #43, 11-87

K88. "`Sci-Fi Prof' Finds Reality" by Doris Byron
Fullerton Daily News Tribune 20-9-76

K89. "Dickian Time in THE MAN IN THE HIGH CASTLE" by Laura E.
Campbell
Extrapolation Vol 33 #3, 1992

K90. "Philip K. Dick Appreciation" by Carol Carr
Locus (fnz) #256, 5-82

K91. Introduction by Glenn Chang
THE WORLD JONES MADE (1979) {Gregg Press edition only}

K92. "DR. BLOODMONEY, OR HOW WE GOT ALONG AFTER THE BOMB"
by E.L. Chapman
SURVEY OF SCIENCE FICTION LITERATURE VOL 2, Magill,
Salem Press, 1979

K93. "BLADE RUNNER, or, The Sociology of Anticipation" by
Yves Chevrier
Science Fiction Studies #32, 3-84

K94. "The Classical Humanism of Philip K. Dick" by Peder
Christiansen
WOMEN WORLDWALKERS, Weedman, Texas Tech Press, 1985

K95. "The Ghost in the Android" by Charles A. Coulombe
Science Fiction Review (fnz) #10, 5-92

K96. Letter by Buck Coulson [response to F22]
SF Commentary (fnz) #41/42, 2-75

K97. "Kafka and Science Fiction" by Istvan Csicsery-Ronay, Jr.
Newsletter of the Kafka Society of America (fnz) #7, 6-83

K98. "Pilgrims in Pandemonium: Philip K. Dick and the Critics"
by Istvan Csicery-Ronay, Jr.
ON PHILIP K. DICK, Mullen/Csicsery-Ronay/Evans/Hollinger,
SF-TH Inc, 1992 {as introduction}

K99. "Philip K. Dick à La Recherche de L'Identité" by
Philip Curval
Le Monde 21-7-78 {in French}

K100. "Philip K. Dick Appreciation" by Avram Davidson
Locus (fnz) #256, 5-82

K101. "Technomancer: Philip K. Dick's Signal Achievements" by
Erik Davis
New York Village Voice 11-7-89

K102. "Philip K. Dick Appreciation" by Grania Davis
      Locus (fnz) #256, 5-82

K103. "PKD and the Versailles Throne" by Grania Davis
      PKDS Newsletter (fnz) #6, 4-85

K104. "Drei Stigmata van Philip K. Dick: of, Is Er Leven Voor
          de Dood?" by Frank R.F. de Cuyper
      JUST THE OTHER DAY, De Vos, Restant, 1985 {in Dutch}

K105. "FLOW, MY TEARS...: Theater and Science Fiction" by
          Samuel R. Delany
      The New York Review of SF (fnz) #1, 9-88

K106. "Het Universum van Philip K. Dick: Een Systeemtheoretische
          Benadering" by Gilbert De Meester
      JUST THE OTHER DAY, De Vos, Restant, 1985 {in Dutch}

K107. Preface to `Jon's World' by August Derleth
      TIME TO COME, Derleth, Farrar, 1954; {not in Berkley
          or Tower editions}

K108. Letter by Anne Dick
      Horizon 12-82

K109. Letter by Anne Dick
      PKDS Newsletter (fnz) #3, 4-84

K110. Letter by Anne Dick
      PKDS Newsletter (fnz) #30, 12-92

K111. Letter by Anne Dick (re Dick biography)
      Locus (fnz) #270, 7-83

K112. Letter by Tessa B. Dick
      Locus (fnz) #271, 8-83

K113. Letter by Tessa B. Dick
      PKDS Newsletter (fnz) #2, 12-83

K114. Letter by Tessa B. Dick
       PKDS Newsletter (fnz) #3, 4-84

K115. Letter by Tessa B. Dick
       PKDS Newsletter (fnz) #17, 4-88

K116. "Letter from Tessa" by Tessa B. Dick
       PKDS Newsletter (fnz) #4, 9-84

K117. "The Search for VALIS" by Tessa B. Dick
       PKDS Newsletter (fnz) #6, 4-85

K118. "I Dreamed I Saw Phil Dick Last Night" by Paul Di Filippo
       The New York Review of SF (fnz) #70, 6-94

K119. Introduction by Thomas M. Disch
       THE LITTLE BLACK BOX / THE EYE OF THE SIBYL (1987)
       WE CAN REMEMBER IT FOR YOU WHOLSESALE (1991) {Grafton
              edition only}

K120. "Cantata 82: An Ode to the Death of Philip K. Dick" (poem)
              by Thomas M. Disch
       Washington Post Book World 23-5-82
       Interzone #2, Summer 1982
       HERE I AM, THERE YOU ARE, WHERE WERE WE? by Thomas M. Disch,
              Poetry Book Society, 1984 {as Ode on the
              Death of Philip K. Dick}

K121. "In the Mold of 1964" by Thomas M. Disch
       THE PENULTIMATE TRUTH (1984) {Bluejay/Carroll & Graf
              editions only}

K122. "Phil Dick: Cult Star in a Martian Sky" by Thomas M. Disch
       Crawdaddy 12-75

K123. "Toward the Transcendent: An Introduction to SOLAR LOTTERY
              and Other Works" by Thomas M. Disch
       SOLAR LOTTERY (1976) {Gregg Press edition only}
       PHILIP K. DICK, Greenberg/Olander, Taplinger, 1983

K124. "BLADE RUNNER and Genre: Film Noir and Science Fiction"
              by Susan Doll & Greg Fuller
       Literature/Film Quarterly Vol 14 #2, 1986

K125. Article by John Dowie [on J27]
       Critical Wave (fnz) #21, -91

K126. "BLADE RUNNER: Science Fiction and Transcendence" by
          David Dresser
       Literature/Film Quarterly #13, 1985

K127. "Do Androids Dream of Ridley Scott?" by David Dresser
       PHOENIX FROM THE ASHES, Yoke, Greenwood, 1987

K128. "The Provocative Adventures of a Major Sci-Fi Writer" by
          Peter C. Du Bois
       Wall Street Journal 8-7-82

K129. "Fame Follows Sci-Fi Author to the Grave" by Alan Dumas
       Rocky Mountain News Sunday Magazine 8-12-91

K130. "Between Faith and Melancholy: Irony and the Gnostic Meaning
          in Dick's `Divine Trilogy'" by Jean-Noël Dumont
       Science-Fiction Studies #45, 7-88 {translated by Danièle
          Chatelain & George Slusser}
       ON PHILIP K. DICK, Mullen/Csicsery-Ronay/Evans/Hollinger,
          SF-TH Inc, 1992 {translated by Danièle
          Chatelain & George Slusser}

K131. "P.K. Dick: From the Death of the Subject to a Theology of
          Late Capitalism" by Scott Durham
       Science-Fiction Studies #45, 7-88
       ON PHILIP K. DICK, Mullen/Csicsery-Ronay/Evans/Hollinger,
          SF-TH Inc, 1992

K132. Letter from Harlan Ellison [in response to K288]
       Foundation #27, 2-83
       Science Fiction Review (fnz) #48, 8-83

K133. Introduction to `Faith of Our Fathers' by Harlan Ellison
       DANGEROUS VISIONS, Ellison, Doubleday, 1967

K134. "California Time-Slip: Philip K. Dick's Memories of
          Irreality" by Steve Erickson
       LA Weekly 9-11-90
       PKDS Newsletter (fnz) #25, 12-90

K135. Introduction by Dennis Etchison
THE SELECTED LETTERS OF PHILIP K. DICK: 1972-1973 (1993)

K136. "Paper World: Science Fiction in the Postmodern Era" by
Welch D. Everman
POSTMODERN FICTION, McCaffrey, Greenwood, 1986

K137. "Fiddlin' with Dick" by Iain Ewing [verse review of VALIS]
Crystal Ship (fnz) #5, 1-82

K138. "VALIS and Wille: An Antinomian Opera" by Christopher Farmer
PKDS Newsletter (fnz) #18, 8-88

K139. "The Transmigration of Philip K. Dick" by John Fekete
[book reviews of PHILIP K. DICK by Hazel Pierce and
PHILIP K. DICK edited by Joseph D. Olander & Martin
H. Greenberg]
Science-Fiction Studies #32, 3-84
ON PHILIP K. DICK, Mullen/Csicsery-Ronay/Evans/Hollinger,
SF-TH Inc, 1992

K140. "Philip K. Dick et/contre La Réalité" by Juan Ignacio Ferrera
Fiction 9-77 {in French}

K141. "Philip K. Dick Made My Brother a Drug Addict" by Ferret
PKDS Newsletter (fnz) #11, 5-86

K142. "BLADE RUNNER and DO ANDROIDS DREAM OF ELECTRIC SHEEP?:
An Ecological Critique of Human-Centred Value
Systems" by Norman Fischer
Canadian Journal of Political and Social Theory
Vol XIII #3, 1989

K143. "Of Living Machines and Living-Machines: BLADE RUNNER and
the Terminal Genre" by William Fisher
New Literary History Vol 20 #1, 1988

K144. Article by Peter Fitting
American Book Review 4/5-92

K145. "Futurecop: The Neutralization of Revolt in BLADE RUNNER"
by Peter Fitting
Science-Fiction Studies #43, 11-87
ON PHILIP K. DICK, Mullen/Csicsery-Ronay/Evans/Hollinger,
SF-TH Inc, 1992

K146. "Philip K. Dick in France" by Peter Fitting
      Science-Fiction Studies #41, 3-87
      ON PHILIP K. DICK, Mullen/Csicsery-Ronay/Evans/Hollinger,
         SF-TH Inc, 1992

K147. "Philip K. Dick is Dead" by Peter Fitting [book review of
         PHILIP K. DICK by Douglas A. Mackey]
      Science-Fiction Studies #48, 7-89
      ON PHILIP K. DICK, Mullen/Csicsery-Ronay/Evans/Hollinger,
         SF-TH Inc, 1992

K148. "Reality as Ideological Construct: A Reading of Five Novels
         by Philip K. Dick" by Peter Fitting
      Science-Fiction Studies #30, 7-83
      La Revue de L'Université Libre de Bruxelles 1983
         {in French, as "Idéologie et Construction
         du Réel Dans L'Oeuvre de Philip K. Dick"}
      ON PHILIP K. DICK, Mullen/Csicsery-Ronay/Evans/Hollinger,
         SF-TH Inc, 1992

K149. Statement by Peter Fitting
      THE SELECTED LETTERS OF PHILIP K. DICK: 1974 (1991)

K150. "UBIK: The Deconstruction of Bourgeois SF" by Peter Fitting
      Science-Fiction Studies #5, 3-75
      PHILIP K. DICK, Greenberg/Olander, Taplinger, 1983
      ON PHILIP K. DICK, Mullen/Csicsery-Ronay/Evans/Hollinger,
         SF-TH Inc, 1992

K151. "Dick, the Libertarian Prophet" by Daniel Fondanèche
      Science-Fiction Studies #45, 7-88 {translated by Danièle
         Chatelain & George Slusser}
      ON PHILIP K. DICK, Mullen/Csicsery-Ronay/Evans/Hollinger,
         SF-TH Inc, 1992 {translated by Danièle
         Chatelain & George Slusser}

K152. "Philip K. Dick: Exile in Paradox" by Cheryl Forbes
      Christianity Today 20-5-77

K153. "In Search of Dick's Boswell" by Carl Freedman [book reviews
         of ONLY APPARENTLY REAL by Paul Williams;
         TO THE HIGH CASTLE: PHILIP K. DICK: A LIFE
         by Gregg Rickman; PKD: A BIBLIOGRAPHY by
         Daniel J.H. Levack & Steven Owen Godersky]
      Science-Fiction Studies #53, 3-91
      ON PHILIP K. DICK, Mullen/Csicsery-Ronay/Evans/Hollinger,
         SF-TH Inc, 1992

K154. "Philip K. Dick and Criticism" by Carl Freedman
Science-Fiction Studies #45, 7-88 {as introduction}
ON PHILIP K. DICK, Mullen/Csicsery-Ronay/Evans/Hollinger,
SF-TH Inc, 1992

K155. "Towards a Theory of Paranoia: The Science Fiction of Philip
K. Dick" by Carl Freedman
Science-Fiction Studies #32, 3-84
ON PHILIP K. DICK, Mullen/Csicsery-Ronay/Evans/Hollinger,
SF-TH Inc, 1992

K156. Afterword by James Frenkel
DR. BLOODMONEY (1985) {Bluejay and Carroll & Graf
editions only}

K157. "Language Fragmentation in Recent Science-Fiction Novels" by
A.J. Frisch
THE INTERSECTION OF SCIENCE FICTION AND PHILOSOPHY, Myers
Greenwood, 1983

K158. "Redemption and Doubt in Philip K. Dick's Valis Trilogy" by
Robert Galbreath
Extrapolation Summer 1983

K159. "Salvation Knowledge: Ironic Gnosticism in VALIS and
FLIGHT TO LUCIFER" by Robert Galbreath
SCIENCE FICTION DIALOGUES, Wolfe, Academy Chicago, 1982

K160. Letter by Russell Galen (on Dick)
PKDS Newsletter (fnz) #5, 12-84

K161. "Philip K. Dick Appreciation" by Russell Galen
Locus (fnz) #256, 5-82
Science Fiction Chronicle (fnz) 5-82

K162. "Hype Anxiety" by Steve Gallagher
Vector (fnz) #110, 1982 (guest editorial)

K163. "First Order, Second Order, Third: Philip K. Dick and
the Varieties of Cybernetics" by Frank Galuszka
Radio Free P.K.D. (fnz) #4, 3-94

K164. "Philip K. Dick Appreciation" by Joseph R. Genovaldi
       Locus (fnz) #256, 5-82

K165. Introduction by William Gibson
       THE SELECTED LETTERS OF PHILIP K. DICK: 1974 (1991)

K166. "Some Blues for Horselover Fat" by William Gibson
       Wing Window (fnz) 3-82

K167. "Philip K. Dick Appreciation" by Daniel Gilbert
       Locus (fnz) #256, 5-82

K168. "THE BEST OF PHILIP K. DICK" by Bruce Gillespie
       SURVEY OF SCIENCE FICTION LITERATURE VOL 1, Magill,
             Salem Press, 1979

K169. "Contradictions" by Bruce Gillespie
       PHILIP K. DICK: ELECTRIC SHEPHERD, Gillespie,
             Norstrilia, 1975

K170. Foreword by Bruce Gillespie
       PHILIP K. DICK: ELECTRIC SHEPHERD, Gillespie,
             Norstrilia, 1975

K171. "Mad, Mad Worlds: Seven Novels of Philip K. Dick" by
             Bruce Gillespie
       SF Commentary (fnz) #1, 1-69
       PHILIP K. DICK: ELECTRIC SHEPHERD, Gillespie,
             Norstrilia, 1975

K172. "Only Apparently Unreal: Deciphering the Novels of Philip
             K. Dick" by Bruce Gillespie
       BRG (fnz) #1, 10-90 {as "The Non-Science Fiction Novels of
             Philip K. Dick: (1928 - 1982)"
       Critical Wave (fnz) #22, 6-91

K173. "Philip K. Dick: The Real Thing" by Bruce Gillespie
       SF Commentary (fnz) #9, 2-70
       PHILIP K. DICK: ELECTRIC SHEPHERD, Gillespie,
             Norstrilia, 1975

K174. Letter by Alexis Gilliland [response to F22]
       SF Commentary (fnz) #41/42, 2-75

K175. "In Remembrance of a Friend's Passing, Philip K. Dick" by
          E.C. Glaser
      Lan's Lantern (fnz) #12, 4-83

K176. Foreword by Steven Owen Godersky
      BEYOND LIES THE WUB (1987) {Underwood-Miller edition only}

K177. "Le Monde Cauchemardesque de PKD" by Jacques Goimard
      Le Monde 1-1-71 {in French}

K178. "An Anecdote" by Lisa Goldstein
      The New York Review of SF (fnz) #70, 6-94

K179. Introduction by Fay Goodlife
      VULCAN'S HAMMER (1979) {Gregg Press edition only}

K180. "THREE STIGMATA OF PALMER ELDRITCH: Critique" by
          Richard Gordon
      Zenith Speculation (fnz) #12, 4-66

K181. "Philip K. Dick: A Parallax View" by Terence M. Green
      Science Fiction Review (fnz) #17, 5-76

K182. "Library Collection Sparks Lawsuit" by Diana Griego
      The Daily Titan 15-9-83

K183. "Will Reality Please Raise its Hand?" by James Gunn
      THE ROAD TO SCIENCE FICTION #3, Gunn, Mentor, 1979

K184. "Philip K. Dick and the PKD Memorial Award" by Marty
          Halpern
      Paperback Parade (fnz) #11, 2-89

K185. "Science Fiction and the American Dream" by William H.
          Hardesty, III
      Essays in Arts and Sciences #9, 1979

K186. Foreword to `A Little Something for Us Tempunauts" by
          David G. Hartwell
      THE DARK DESCENT, Hartwell, Tor, 1987; Grafton, 1990
          (17 of 56, as THE DARK DESCENT: A FABULOUS
          FORMLESS DARKNESS);

K187. Introduction by David G. Hartwell
      COUNTER-CLOCK WORLD (1979) {Gregg Press edition only}

K188. Introduction to `The Indefatigible Frog' by David G. Hartwell
      The New York Review of SF (fnz) #68, 4-94
      THE ASCENT OF WONDER, Hartwell/Cramer, Tor, 1994

K189. "The Special Philip K. Dick Issue" by David G. Hartwell
      The New York Review of SF (fnz) #70, 6-94 {as editorial}

K190. "Metaphysics and Metafiction in THE MAN IN THE HIGH CASTLE"
           by N.B. Hayles
      PHILIP K. DICK, Greenberg/Olander, Taplinger, 1983

K191. "A Report on the Western Front: Postmodernism and the
           `Politics' of style" by Dick Hebdige
      Block Winter 1986/87

K192. "Gedanke an Den Tod" by Christian Hederer
      Quarber Merkur (fnz) #60, 12-83 {in German}

K193. "One Hundred Most Important People in Science Fiction/
           Fantasy: Philip K. Dick" by Chris Henderson
      Starlog #100, 11-85

K194. Entry by P.G. Hogan, Jr.
      TWENTIETH-CENTURY SCIENCE-FICTION WRITERS, PART 1: A-L,
           Cowart, Gale, 1981

K195. "Philip K. Dick: Authenticity and Insincerity" by John
           Huntingdon
      Science-Fiction Studies #45, 7-88
      ON PHILIP K. DICK, Mullen/Csicsery-Ronay/Evans/Hollinger,
           SF-TH Inc, 1992

K196. Foreword by Mark Hurst
      THE GOLDEN MAN (1980)

K197. "Last Contact" by Mark Hurst
      PKDS Newsletter (fnz) #3, 4-84

K198. "Can We All Get Along?" by David Hyde
       Radio Free P.K.D. (fnz) #1, 2-93

K199. "Philip K. Dick - Charting the Unreal: Science Fiction's
           Tormented Genius" by Dave Hyde
       Territories (fnz) #4, Summer 1994

K200. "Ridley Scott and Philip K. Dick" by Jake Jakaitis [book
           review of RETROFITTING BLADE RUNNER by Judith P.
           Kerman]
       Science-Fiction Studies #57, 1992
       ON PHILIP K. DICK, Mullen/Csicsery-Ronay/Evans/Hollinger,
           SF-TH Inc, 1992

K201. Afterword by Maxim Jakubowski
       THE ZAP GUN (1984) {Bluejay and Carroll & Graf
           editions only}

K202. "Flow My Tears, the Writer Said. A Farewell to Philip K.
           Dick" by Maxim Jakubowski & Malcolm Edwards
       New Musical Express 13-3-82

K203. "After Armageddon: Character Systems in DR. BLOODMONEY" by
           Fredric Jameson
       Science-Fiction Studies #5, 3-75
       ON PHILIP K. DICK, Mullen/Csicsery-Ronay/Evans/Hollinger,
           SF-TH Inc, 1992

K204. "Nostalgia for the Future" by Fredric Jameson
       South Atlantic Quarterly #88, Spring 1989 {as "Nostalgia
           for the Present"}
       POSTMODERNISM OR, THE CULTURAL LOGIC OF LATE CAPITALISM
           by Frederic Jameson, Verso, 1991

K205. "Phil's Cat" by K.W. Jeter
       Last Wave #3, Summer 1984

K206. "How `Dickian' is the New French Science Fiction?" by
           Emmanuel Joanne
       Science-Fiction Studies #45, 7-88 {translated by Danièle
           Chatelain & George Slusser}
       ON PHILIP K. DICK, Mullen/Csicsery-Ronay/Evans/Hollinger,
           SF-TH Inc, 1992 {translated by Danièle
           Chatelain & George Slusser}

K207. "Roog-na! Roog-na! An Interview with Martin Roogna"
          by Eric A. Johnson
      Radio Free P.K.D. (fnz) #4, 3-94

K208. "My Favourite Time-Slips of Science Fiction! - A Survey"
          by Stig W. Jorgensen
      Mythomania (fnz) #5, 1990

K209. "Philip K. Dick & The Illuminati" by Jay Katz
      Steamshovel Press #8, 1993

K210. "From Pessimism to Sentimentality: DO ANDROIDS DREAM OF
          ELECTRIC SHEEP? becomes BLADE RUNNER" by
          Philip E. Kaveny
      PATTERNS OF THE FANTASTIC II, Hassler, Starmont, 1985

K211. "Space to Believe, Time to Confess" by Roz Kaveney
      unknown UK magazine
      PKDS Newsletter #1, 8-83 {extract}

K212. "Was PKD a Flake?" by John Keel
      PKDS Newsletter (fnz) #15, 8-87

K213. "Science Fiction and the Gothic" by Thomas H. Keeling
      BRIDGES TO SCIENCE FICTION, Slusser/Guffey/Rose,
          Southern Illinois University Press, 1980

K214. Letter by David Keller (re: molestation of Dick as child)
      PKDS Newsletter (fnz) #24, 5-90

K215. "The Time Machine: Philip K. Dick, The Middle Period" by
          George Kelley
      Paperback Quarterly (fnz) Vol 2 #1, Spring 1979

K216. "Private Eye: A Semiotic Comparison of the film BLADE RUNNER
          and the book DO ANDROIDS DREAM OF ELECTRIC SHEEP"
          by Judith B. Kerman
      PATTERNS OF THE FANTASTIC II, Hassler, Starmont, 1985
      [expanded as M9, 1991]

K217. "Broken Bubbles: The Progress of Philip K. Dick from
          Mainstream to SF" by Paul Kincaid [reviews of
          THE BROKEN BUBBLE and OUR FRIENDS FROM FROLIX 8]
      Vector (fnz) #153, 12-89/1-90

K218. "The Mysterious Gnosis of Philip K. Dick" by Jay Kinney
      Critique #11/12, Spring/Summer 1983
      Gnosis (fnz) #1, Fall/Winter 1985 {revised as "The
          Mysterious Revelations of Philip K. Dick"}

K219. "Summary of the Exegesis based on Preliminary Forays" by
          Jay Kinney
      PKDS Newsletter (fnz) #3, 4-84
      PHILIP K. DICK: THE LAST TESTAMENT by Gregg Rickman,
          Fragments West, 1985

K220. "Wrestling with Angels: The Mystical Dilemma of Philip K.
          Dick" by Jay Kinney
      IN PURSUIT OF VALIS: SELECTIONS FROM THE EXEGESIS (1991)

K221. "Concerning Pages Arising from Nothingness..." by Gérard Klein
      FLOW MY TEARS, THE POLICEMAN SAID (1985) {Laffont edition
          only} {in French}
      PKDS Newsletter (fnz) #28, 3-92 {translated by Paul
          Williams}

K222. "Philip K. Dick Appreciation" by Gérard Klein
      Locus (fnz) #256, 5-82

K223. "Philip K. Dick ou L'Amérique Schizophrène" by Gérard Klein
      Fiction #182, 2-69 {in French}

K224. "Le Point de Vue Littéraire" by Gérard Klein
      L'OEIL DANS LE CIEL (1958) {in French, as preface}

K225. "Philip K. Dick Appreciation" by Damon Knight
      Locus (fnz) #256, 5-82

K226. "BLADE RUNNER may mean a Second Coming for Sci-Fi Marvel
          Philip K. Dick" by Steven Kosek
      Chicago Tribune 4/7/82
      NEWSBANK LITERATURE #9, 1982/83

K227. "Staying Alive in a Fifteen Cent Universe" by Claudia Krenz
          [shortened version of M5]
      SF Commentary (fnz) #62/63/64/65/66, 6-81

K228. "Paperback Writer: The Ubiquitous World of Philip K. Dick"
          by Lars Kyrie
      Amazing Experiences 11-90

K229. "The Last Testament of Philip K. Dick" by David Lagraff
          & Sean Elder
      The Berkeley Monthly 8-85

K230. "My Luncheon with Philip" by Marc Laidlaw
      The New York Review of SF (fnz) #70, 6-94

K231. Letter by Ken Lake [on K172]
      Critical Wave (fnz) #23, 1991

K232. Obituary by Dave Langford
      Extro #2, 4/5-82

K233. "Philip Kendred Dick (1928-1982)" by Fazekas László
      Galaktika #52, 1983 {in Hungarian}

K234. "DO ANDROIDS DREAM OF ELECTRIC SHEEP?" by Donald L. Lawler
      SURVEY OF SCIENCE FICTION LITERATURE VOL 2, Magill,
          Salem Press, 1979

K235. "Philip K. Dick: Un Contrebandier de la Science-Fiction" by
          David Le Breton
      Esprit #10, 7-88

K236. Letter by Ursula K. Le Guin (on Dick)
      Foundation #27, 2-83

K237. "Philip K. Dick Appreciation" by Ursula K. Le Guin
      Locus (fnz) #256, 5-82

K238. "Science Fiction as Prophesy: Philip K. Dick" by Ursula
          K. Le Guin
      The New Republic 30-10-76
      THE LANGUAGE OF THE NIGHT by Ursula K. Le Guin,
          Putnam, 1979 {as "The Modest One"}

K239. "Barjo Premieres in the USA" by Greg Lee
      Radio Free P.K.D. (fnz) #3, 10-93

K240. "From Beyond the Grave" by Gregory Lee
        Orange Coast 8-91

K241. "PKD: 2193 A.D." by Greg Lee, Michael Bishop, Thomas
            Disch, Tim Powers, John Shirley, Robert
            Silverberg & Ernesto Spinelli
        Radio Free P.K.D. (fnz) #2, 5-93

K242. "A Short, Happy Visit from the BBC" by Greg Lee [on J22]
        Radio Free P.K.D. (fnz) #3, 10-93

K243. "Why I Dig PKD" by Gregory Lee
        The New York Review of SF (fnz) #70, 6-94

K244. "Philip K. Dick: a Visionary among the Charlatans" by
            Stanislaw Lem
        Science Fiction Studies #5, 3-75 {translated from the
            Polish by Robert Abernathy}
        SCIENCE FICTION STUDIES - SELECTED ARTICLES IN SCIENCE
            FICTION 1973-75, Mullen/Suvin, Boston, 1976
                {translated from the Polish by Robert Abernathy}
        MICROWORLDS by Stanislaw Lem, Harcourt, 1984
        ON PHILIP K. DICK, Mullen/Csicsery-Ronay/Evans/Hollinger,
            SF-TH Inc, 1992 {translated from the Polish
            by Robert Abernathy}

K245. "Science and Reality in Philip K. Dick's UBIK" by
            Stanislaw Lem
        Quarber Merkur (fnz) #30 {translated into German by
            Werner Koopman}
        SF Commentary (fnz) #35/36/37, 7/8/9-73
        MULTITUDE OF VISIONS, Chauvin, T-K Graphics, 1975

K246. "Science Fiction: A Hopeless Case - with Exceptions" by
            Stanislaw Lem
        FANTASTYKA I FUTUROLOGIA by Stanislaw Lem, Krakow, 1973 {in
            Polish, as "Philip K. Dick, Czyli Fantomatyka
            Mimo Woli"}
        Quarber Merkur (fnz) #30 {translated into German by Werner
            Koopman, as "Science Fiction: Ein Hoffnungloser
            Fall - Mit Ausnahmen"}
        SF Commentary (fnz) #35/36/37, 7/8/9-73
        PHILIP K. DICK: ELECTRIC SHEPHERD, Gillespie,
            Norstrilia, 1975

K247. Statement by Stanislaw Lem
THE SELECTED LETTERS OF PHILIP K. DICK: 1974 (1991)

K248. "Conformity in Science Fiction" by Bill Leman
Inside Science Fiction (fnz) #52, 10-75

K249. "Two Dickian Novels" by Jonathan Lethem
PKDS Newsletter (fnz) #24, 5-90

K250. "The Unexpurgated ZAP GUN: A Report" by Jonathan Lethem
PKDS Newsletter (fnz) #15, 8-87

K251. Letter from Linda Levy/Taylor
PKDS Newsletter (fnz) #20, 4-89

K252. "More on P.K. Dick" by Shawn Loudermilk
Paperback Quarterly Fall 1982

K253. Introduction by Richard A. Lupoff
A HANDFUL OF DARKNESS (1978) {Gregg Press edition only}

K254. "Philip K. Dick Appreciation" by Richard A. Lupoff
Locus (fnz) #256, 5-82

K255. "A Rainy Afternoon with Phil and Joan" by Richard A. Lupoff
The New York Review of SF (fnz) #70, 6-94

K256. "The Realities of Philip K. Dick" by Richard A. Lupoff
Starship (fnz) Vol 16 #3, Summer 1979

K257. "Philip K. Dick and The Perception of Reality, or, New
Weltanschauungs for Old" by Lesleigh Luttrell
Janus Vol 3 #1, Spring 1977

K258. "The Really Real" by Lesleigh Luttrell
SF Commentary #62/63/64/65/66, 6-81

K259. "Philip K. Dick" by Kevin Lyons
The Edge (fnz) #2, 3/4-90

K260. "VALIS - the Opera" (press release) by Tod Machover
        PKDS Newsletter (fnz) #15, 8-87 {extract}

K261. "EYE IN THE SKY" by Douglas Mackey
        SURVEY OF SCIENCE FICTION LITERATURE VOL 2, Magill,
            Salem Press, 1979

K262. "Science Fiction and Gnosticism" by Douglas Mackey
        The Missouri Review Vol VII #2, 1984

K263. "Philip Dick's THE MAN IN THE HIGH CASTLE and the Nature of
            Science-Fictional Worlds" by Carl D. Malmgren
        BRIDGES TO SCIENCE FICTION, Slusser/Guffey/Rose,
            Southern Illinois University Press, 1980

K264. Afterword by Barry N. Malzberg
        CLANS OF THE ALPHANE MOON (1984) {Bluejay/Carroll & Graf
            editions only}

K265. "Philip K. Dick" by Barry N. Malzberg
        PHILIP K. DICK, Greenberg/Olander, Taplinger, 1983
            {as introduction}

K266. "Influence of Science Fiction in the Contemporary American
            Novel" by Kenneth Mathieson
        Science Fiction Studies #35, 3-85

K267. "I Understand Philip K. Dick" by Terence McKenna
        IN PURSUIT OF VALIS: SELECTIONS FROM THE EXEGESIS (1991)

K268. "THE MAN IN THE HIGH CASTLE" by Willis E. McNelly
        SURVEY OF SCIENCE FICTION LITERATURE VOL 3, Magill,
            Salem Press, 1979

K269. "Philip K. Dick Manuscripts and Books: the Manuscripts at
            Fullerton" by Willis E. McNelly
        Science Fiction Studies #5, 3-75
        ON PHILIP K. DICK, Mullen/Csicsery-Ronay/Evans/Hollinger,
            SF-TH Inc, 1992 {updated & expanded by Sharon K. Perry}

K270. "PKD and Me" by Ed Meskys
        Niekas (fnz) #34, 1986

K271. Introduction by Sandra Miesel
        EYE IN THE SKY (1979) {Gregg Press edition only}

K272. Introduction by Joseph Milicia
        THE MAN IN THE HIGH CASTLE (1979) {Gregg Press edition only}

K273. "The Philip K. Dick Issue of Science Fiction Studies"
            by Joseph Milicia
        The New York Review of SF (fnz) #7, 3-89

K274. "BLADE RUNNER" by Tom Milne
        Monthly Film Bulletin #584, 1982

K275. "The Real Ideas of Philip K. Dick" by Michael Moorcock
        Vector (fnz) #39, 4-66

K276. "Casablanca meets Star Wars: The Blakean Dialectics of
            BLADE RUNNER" by Rachela Morrison
        Literature/Film Quarterly Vol 18 #1, 1990

K277. "Media, Messages and Myths: Three Fictionists for the
            Near Future" by Jose M. Mota
        STORM WARNINGS, SLusser, Southern Illinois University
            Press, 1987

K278. "Books, Stories, Essays" by R.D. Mullen
        Science Fiction Studies #5, 3-75

K279. "The Word According to Dick" by Paul S. Nathan (about Dick's
            refusal to novelize BLADE RUNNER)
        Publishers Weekly 18-6-82

K280. "Philip K. Dick" by Keith Neilson
        CRITICAL SURVEY OF SHORT FICTION, Magill, Salem Press, 1981

K281. "UBIK" by Keith Neilson
        SURVEY OF SCIENCE FICTION LITERATURE VOL 5, Magill,
            Salem Press, 1979

K282. "An Appreciation" by Kirsten Nelson
        Last Wave 10-83

K283. "A Dream of Amerasia" by R. Faraday Nelson
        PHILIP K. DICK: THE DREAM CONNECTION, Apel,
            Permanent Press, 1987

K284. "Philip K. Dick and the Two Bookstores" by Ray Nelson
        PKDS Newsletter (fnz) #26, 4-91

K285. "Philip K. Dick Appreciation" by R. Faraday Nelson
        Locus (fnz) #256, 5-82

K286. "At `The Strange Pilgrimage': A Commemoration for Philip
            K. Dick (1928-82)" by Joseph Nicholas
        Ansible (fnz) 1982

K287. Introduction to `Man, Android and Machine' by Peter Nicholls
        SCIENCE FICTION AT LARGE, Nicholls, Gollancz, 1976;
            Fontana, 1978 (as EXPLORATIONS OF THE MARVELLOUS);

K288. "Philip K. Dick: A Cowardly Memoir" by Peter Nicholls
        Talk at the City Literary Institute, London, 9-6-82
        Tappen (fnz) #4, 6-82
        Foundation #26, 10-82
        Science Fiction Review (fnz) #47, 5-83

K289. "Dick and Meta-SF" by Carlo Pagetti
        Science-Fiction Studies #5, 3-75
        ON PHILIP K. DICK, Mullen/Csicsery-Ronay/Evans/Hollinger,
            SF-TH Inc, 1992

K290. "Critique and Fantasy in Two Novels by Philip K. Dick"
            by Christopher Palmer
        Extrapolation Vol 32 #3, Fall 1991

K291. "The Last Post: Science Fiction and the Posthuman"
            by Christopher Palmer
        Arena (fnz) #3, 2/3-93

K292. "Postmodernism and the Birth of the Author in VALIS"
            by Christopher Palmer
        Science-Fiction Studies #55, 11-91
        ON PHILIP K. DICK, Mullen/Csicsery-Ronay/Evans/Hollinger,
            SF-TH Inc, 1992

K293. "A SCANNER DARKLY and Postmodernsim" by Christopher Palmer
       Arena (fnz) #92, 1991

K294. "Greater Than Heinlein" by Bob Parkinson
       Speculation (fnz) #21, 2-69

K295. Bibliography by Fred Patten
       PHILIP K. DICK: ELECTRIC SHEPHERD, Gillespie,
             Norstrilia, 1975

K296. "The Unreconstructed Man: The Fiction of Philip K. Dick" by
             Jeffrey W. Peacock
       Dissertations Abstracts International 9-90

K297. "Author Checklist No. 7 - Philip K. Dick" by Rog Peyton
       Andromeda Book Co. Catalogue #13, 1-72

K298. "The Two Faces of Philip K. Dick" by Robert M. Philmus
             {incl extracts from 2 Dick letters}
       Science-Fiction Studies #53, 3-91
       ON PHILIP K. DICK, Mullen/Csicsery-Ronay/Evans/Hollinger,
             SF-TH Inc, 1992

K299. "FLOW MY TEARS, THE POLICEMAN SAID" by Hazel Pierce
       SURVEY OF SCIENCE FICTION LITERATURE VOL 2, Magill,
             Salem Press, 1979

K300. "Philip K. Dick's Political Dream" by Hazel Pierce
       PHILIP K. DICK, Greenberg/Olander, Taplinger, 1983

K301. "Do Androids Dream of Philip K. Dick" by Charles Platt
       Horizon 7/8-82

K302. Introduction by Charles Platt
       THE ZAP GUN (1979) {Gregg Press edition only}

K303. Letter by Charles Platt [in response to K288]
       Science Fiction Review (fnz) #48, 8-83

K304. "Philip K. Dick" by Charles Platt [obituary]
       The Patchin Review (fnz) #4, 4/6-82

K305. "Philip K. Dick Appreciation" by Frederik Pohl
        Locus (fnz) #256, 5-82

K306. Introduction to `Rautavaara's Case' by Jerry Pournelle
        NEBULA AWARD STORIES 16, Pournelle/Carr,
            Holt, Rinehart & Winston, 1982

K307. Foreword by Tim Powers
        UBIK: THE SCREENPLAY (1985)

K308. Introduction by Tim Powers
        THE BROKEN BUBBLE (1988) {Ultramarine edition only}

K309. "The Death of Philip K. Dick" by Tim Powers
        PKDS Newsletter (fnz) #3, 4-84

K310. Introduction by Tim Powers
        THE SELECTED LETTERS OF PHILIP K. DICK: 1975-1976 (1992)

K311. "Philip K. Dick Appreciation" by Tim Powers
        Locus (fnz) #256, 5-82

K312. "Some Random Memories of Philip K. Dick" by Tim Powers
        PKDS Newsletter (fnz) #2, 12-83

K313. "Some Random Notes on VALIS and Philip K. Dick's Mystical
            Experiences" by Tim Powers
        PKDS Newsletter (fnz) #4, 9-84

K314. "DO ANDROIDS DREAM OF ELECTRIC SHEEP?" by David Pringle
        SCIENCE FICTION: THE 100 BEST NOVELS, Pringle, Xanadu, 1985

K315. "DR. BLOODMONEY" by David Pringle
        SCIENCE FICTION: THE 100 BEST NOVELS, Pringle, Xanadu, 1985

K316. "THE MAN IN THE HIGH CASTLE" by David Pringle
        SCIENCE FICTION: THE 100 BEST NOVELS, Pringle, Xanadu, 1985

K317. "MARTIAN TIME-SLIP" by David Pringle
        SCIENCE FICTION: THE 100 BEST NOVELS, Pringle, Xanadu, 1985

K318. "THE THREE STIGMATA OF PALMER ELDRITCH" by David Pringle
       SCIENCE FICTION: THE 100 BEST NOVELS, Pringle, Xanadu, 1985

K319. "TIME OUT OF JOINT" by David Pringle
       SCIENCE FICTION: THE 100 BEST NOVELS, Pringle, Xanadu, 1985

K320. "Even Sheep can Upset Scientific Detachment" by Philip Purser
       Daily Telegraph Magazine 19-7-74

K321. "Irrational Expectations: or, How Economics and the Post-
             Industrial World Failed Philip K. Dick" by
             Eric S. Rabkin
       Science-Fiction Studies #45, 7-88
       ON PHILIP K. DICK, Mullen/Csicsery-Ronay/Evans/Hollinger,
             SF-TH Inc, 1992

K322. Article by Michael Rapoport
       Republican-American 24-6-90

K323. Entry by Robert Reginald
       CONTEMPORARY SCIENCE FICTION AUTHORS II, Reginald,
             Gale, 1979

K324. "The PKDS Interview with Tessa B. Dick (and Christopher
             Dick)" by J.B. Reynolds
       PKDS Newsletter #13, 2-87

K325. "The PKDS Interview with Tim Powers and James P. Blaylock"
             by J.B. Reynolds and Andy Watson
       PKDS Newsletter #8, 9-85

K326. "Dick, Deception, and Dissociation: A Comment on
             `The Two Faces of Philip K. Dick'"
             by Gregg Rickman [on K298]
       Science-Fiction Studies #54, 7-91
       ON PHILIP K. DICK, Mullen/Csicsery-Ronay/Evans/Hollinger,
             SF-TH Inc, 1992

K327. Introduction to "The Riddle of TLE" [O14] by Gregg Rickman
       PKDS Newsletter (fnz) #20, 4-89

K328. Letter by Gregg Rickman (on the grounds for his claim that
             Dick was molested as a child)
       PKDS Newsletter (fnz) #24, 5-90

K329. "The Nature of Dick's Fantasies" by Gregg Rickman [book
          reviews of IN PURSUIT OF VALIS and THE SELECTED
          LETTERS OF PHILIP K. DICK: 1974]
       Science-Fiction Studies #56, 3-92
       ON PHILIP K. DICK, Mullen/Csicsery-Ronay/Evans/Hollinger,
          SF-TH Inc, 1992

K330. "Philip K. Dick and the Search for Caritas" by Gregg Rickman
       PHILIP K. DICK: IN HIS OWN WORDS by Gregg Rickman,
          Fragments West, 1984

K331. "Phil's Cats" by Gregg Rickman
       PKDS Newsletter #15, 8-87

K332. "A Visit with Philip K. Dick" by Gregg Rickman
       Uncle Jam International (fnz) 7-81
       PHILIP K. DICK: IN HIS OWN WORDS by Gregg Rickman,
          Fragments West, 1984

K333. "What the Quizmaster Took" by Gregg Rickman
       PKDS Newsletter (fnz) #21, 9-89

K334. "The Metafictive World of THE MAN IN THE HIGH CASTLE:
          Hermeneutics, Ethics and Political Ideology"
          by John Rieder
       Science-Fiction Studies #45, 7-88
       ON PHILIP K. DICK, Mullen/Csicsery-Ronay/Evans/Hollinger,
          SF-TH Inc, 1992

K335. "Philip Kindred Dick: A Checklist of U.S. and British
          Paperbacks" by Hal Roberts
       Books Are Everything (fnz) #16, Winter 1990

K336. Afterword by Kim Stanley Robinson
       VALIS (1987) {Kerosina editions only}
       Thrust (fnz) #31, Fall 1988
       THE VALIS TRILOGY (1989)

K337. Interview with Kim Stanley Robinson (on Dick's influence)
       Critical Wave (fnz) #29

K338. "Whose `Failure of Scholarship?'" by Kim Stanley
          Robinson (letter) [on K35]
       Science-Fiction Studies #41, 3-87
       ON PHILIP K. DICK, Mullen/Csicsery-Ronay/Evans/Hollinger,
          SF-TH Inc, 1992

K339. "Phil Dick Lives" by Rudy Rucker
PKDS Newsletter (fnz) #4, 9-84

K340. "Remembering Philip K. Dick" by Alan Ryan
Fantasy Newsletter (fnz) #49, 7-82

K341. "Philip K. Dick: A Play" by Geoff Ryman [review of J27]
The Intermediate Reptile (fnz) #3, 1989

K342. "To the Spirit of Philip K. Dick" by Sachiko
Trap Door (fnz) -84
PKDS Newsletter (fnz) #3, 4-84

K343. "The Making of Blade Runner" by Paul Sammon
Cinefantastique 7/8-82

K344. "Reading: Requiem for a Crap Artist" by Lee Sandlin
Reader (?) 17-9-82

K345. "The Transmigration of Philip K. Dick" by Gregory Sandow
Village Voice Literary Supplement 8-82
PKDS Newsletter #1, 8-83 {extract}

K346. "Past is Present" by Doris Elaine Sauter [review of J24]
PKDS Newsletter (fnz) #26, 4-91

K347. "The Apochryphal Judaic Traditions as Historic Repertoire.
An Analysis of THE DIVINE INVASION by Philip K.
Dick" by Georg Schmidt
Degres Revuew de Synthese a Orientation Semiologique #51,
Autumn 1987

K348. "`I'm Not in the Business, I am the Business': Women at
Work in Hollywood Science Fiction" by Erica Sheen
WHERE NO MAN HAS GONE BEFORE, Armitt, Routledge, 1991

K349. "First Impressions of TOTAL RECALL" by John Shirley
PKDS Newsletter (fnz) #25, 12-90

K350. Introduction by Robert Silverberg
CLANS OF THE ALPHANE MOON (1979) {Gregg Press edition only}

K351. Introduction by Robert Silverberg
    PHILIP K. DICK: THE LAST TESTAMENT by Gregg Rickman,
        Fragments West, 1985

K352. "`Colony': I Trusted the Rug Completely" by Robert Silverberg
    ROBERT SILVERBERG'S WORLDS OF WONDER, Silverberg,
        Warner, 1987

K353. "Philip K. Dick Appreciation" by Robert Silverberg
    Locus (fnz) #256, 5-82

K354. "The Power of Small Things in Philip K. Dick's THE MAN IN
        THE HIGH CASTLE" by John L. Simons
    The Rocky Mountain Review of Language and Literature
        Vol 39 #4, 1985

K355. "Romanticizing Cybernetics in Ridley Scott's BLADE RUNNER"
        by Joseph W. Slade
    Literature/Film Quarterly Vol 18 #1, 1990

K356. "History, Historicity, Story" by George Slusser
    Science-Fiction Studies #45, 7-88
    ON PHILIP K. DICK, Mullen/Csicsery-Ronay/Evans/Hollinger,
        SF-TH Inc, 1992

K357. "Scholars and Pedants" by George Slusser (letter) [on
        K35 and K338]
    Science-Fiction Studies #42, 7-87
    ON PHILIP K. DICK, Mullen/Csicsery-Ronay/Evans/Hollinger,
        SF-TH Inc, 1992

K358. "Philip K. Dick: The Greatest Novels" by David Alexander
        Smith, Kathryn Cramer, Paul Di Filippo, David G.
        Hartwell, Alexander Jablokov & Eric Van
    panel at the 1st American Philip K. Dick Convention,
        Cambridge, Massachusetts, 25-Sep-1993
    The New York Review of SF (fnz) #70, 6-94

K359. "Destination Without End: Philip K. Dick's `I Hope I Shall
        Arrive Soon'" by Steve Sneyd
    SF Spectrum Extra (fnz) 7-86

K360. "Dick Soup" by Steve Sneyd {on slapstick elements in Dick}
    Transylvanian Brain Surgery (fnz) #5, 1977

K361. "Where the People are as Strange as Spaceships" by Steve
        Sneyd [review of IN MILTON LUMKY TERRITORY]
        SF Spectrum Extra (fnz) #6, 1985

K362. "Seven Panels of Dick in Depth" by Ned Sonntag (cartoons
        based on and introducing Dick's work)
        Heavy Metal 9-83

K363. Letter by Dr. Ernesto Spinelli [reply to K70]
        The Guardian 28-7-90

K364. "Spinelli's Speculative Synchronicities" by Dr. Ernesto
        Spinelli
        PHILIP K. DICK: A CELEBRATION, Merrifield/Joyce,
            Connections, 1991
        PKDS Newsletter (fnz) #28, 3-92 {as "Philip K. Dick and
            the Philosophy of Uncertainty"}

K365. Introduction by Norman Spinrad
        DR. BLOODMONEY (1977) {Gregg Press edition only}

K366. Introduction by Norman Spinrad
        SECOND VARIETY (1987) {not in Citadel Twilight edition}
        WE CAN REMEMBER IT FOR YOU WHOLESALE (1990)
            {Citadel Twilight edition only}

K367. "Philip K. Dick Appreciation" by Norman Spinrad
        Science Fiction Chronicle (fnz) 5-82

K368. "The Transmogrification of Philip K. Dick" by Norman Spinrad
        SCIENCE FICTION IN THE REAL WORLD by Norman Spinrad,
            Southern Illinois University Press, 1990

K369. Entry by Brian Stableford
        THE ENCYCLOPEDIA OF SCIENCE FICTION, Nicholls,
            Granada, 1979

K370. Entry by Brian Stableford & John Clute
        THE ENCYCLOPEDIA OF SCIENCE FICTION, Clute/Nicholls,

K371. Entry by Brian Stableford
        SCIENCE FICTION WRITERS, Bleiler, Scribners, 1982

K372. "THE THREE STIGMATA OF PALMER ELDRITCH" by Brian Stableford
      SURVEY OF SCIENCE FICTION LITERATURE VOL 5, Magill,
            Salem Press, 1979

K373. "Fullerton's Philip K. Dick: Science Fiction: It's About
            Today, not Tomorrow" by Richard A. Staley
      Fullerton Daily News Tribune 3-3-82

K374. Introduction/Afterword by Lou Stathis
      TIME OUT OF JOINT (1979) {Gregg Press, Bluejay and Carroll
            & Graf editions only}

K375. Obituary by Lou Stathis
      Heavy Metal ??-82 [references suggest 5-82, but not in
            that issue]

K376. "Philip K. Dick is (Still) Dead: The Death, Resurrection and
            Apotheosis of the Cranky Guru, One Decade On" by
            Lou Stathis
      Reflex #23, 3-92

K377. "Do Replicants Dream of Philip K. Dick" by Bhob Stewart
      Comics Journal #76, 10-82
      PKDS Newsletter (fnz) #3, 4-84 {extract}

K378. "Mystical Healing: Reading Philip K. Dick's VALIS and THE
            DIVINE INVASION as Metapsychoanalytical Novels" by
            Roger J. Stilling
      South Atlantic Review 5-91

K379. "The Age of the Replicant" by Philip Strick
      Sight and Sound Vol 51 #2, 1982

K380. "Philip K. Dick and the Movies" by Philip Strick
      Talk at the City Literary Institute, London, 9-6-82
      Foundation #26, 10-82

K381. "Theodore Sturgeon on Philip K. Dick" by Theodore Sturgeon
      PHILIP K. DICK: THE DREAM CONNECTION, Apel,
            Permanent Press, 1987

K382. "What Do They See in Philip K. Dick" by Tony Sudbery
      Speculation (fnz) #29, 10-71

K383. "To Praise, and not to Bury" by Timothy Robert Sullivan
            [review of THE TRANSMIGRATION OF TIMOTHY ARCHER]
         Fantasy Newsletter #51, 9-82

K384. "Notes from a Low-Budget Stage Director" by Dan Sutherland
         PKDS Newsletter (fnz) #22/23, 12-89

K385. "Confessions of a Philip K. Dick Biographer" by Lawrence Sutin
         PKDS Newsletter (fnz) #22/23, 12-89

K386. "On the Exegesis of Philip K. Dick" by Lawrence Sutin
         IN PURSUIT OF VALIS: SELECTIONS FROM THE EXEGESIS (1991)

K387. "The Opus: Artifice as Refuge and World View" by Darko Suvin
         Science-Fiction Studies #5, 3-75
         PHILIP K. DICK, Greenberg/Olander, Taplinger, 1983 {revised}
         ON PHILIP K. DICK, Mullen/Csicsery-Ronay/Evans/Hollinger,
            SF-TH Inc, 1992

K388. "The Science Fiction of Philip K. Dick" by Darko Suvin
         Science-Fiction Studies #5, 3-75 {as editorial}
         ON PHILIP K. DICK, Mullen/Csicsery-Ronay/Evans/Hollinger,
            SF-TH Inc, 1992 {as introductory note}

K389. "Eight Takes on Kindred Themes" by Michael Swanwick
         The New York Review of SF (fnz) #70, 6-94

K390. "Can God Fly? Can He Hold Out His Arms and Fly? The Fiction
            of Philip K. Dick" by Angus Taylor
         Foundation #4, 7-73

K391. Letter by Angus Taylor [on Dick]
         Foundation #27, 2-83

K392. Letter by Angus Taylor [on Dick and Science Fiction Studies]
         Foundation #60, Spring 1994

K393. "Philip K. Dick and the Psychogenic Origins of Death by
            Meteor-Strike" by Angus Taylor
         Energumen (fnz) #13, 9-72

K394. "The Politics of Space, Time and Entropy" by Angus Taylor
SF Commentary (fnz) #44/45, 12-75
Foundation #10, 6-76

K395. "Entering the World of Philip K. Dick" by John W. Taylor
Tales of the Unanticipated Fall 1986

K396. Bibliography by Marcel Thaon
LE LIVRE D'OR DE LA SCIENCE-FICTION PHILIP K. DICK (1979)

K397. "Dick et ses Fantasmes, ou Lisant la Bible Psychédelique"
by Marcel Thaon
Fiction #190, 10-69 {in French}

K398. "Labyrinthe de Mort" by Marcel Thaon
LE LIVRE D'OR DE LA SCIENCE-FICTION PHILIP K. DICK (1979)
{as Preface, in French}

K399. "Contributions to a Crap Artist" by Jurgen Thomann
Fandom Newsletter (fnz) 8-91 {in German}

K400. "Confessions of a Moviegoer" [film review of CONFESSIONS
D'UN BARJO] by Pascal J. Thomas
PKDS Newsletter (fnz) #29, 9-92

K401. "French SF and the Legacy of Philip K. Dick" by
Pascal J. Thomas
Foundation #34, Autumn 1985

K402. Introduction by Robert Thurston
THE GAME-PLAYERS OF TITAN (1979) {Gregg Press edition only}

K403. "Divinely Inspired" [interview with Lawrence Sutin] by
Andrew Tidmarsh
Interzone #56, 2-92

K404. "A Genius Darkly" by James Tiptree, Jr. {letter to Ted White}
The New York Review of Science Fiction (fnz) #63, 11-93

K405. "How Do You Know You're Reading Philip K. Dick?" by
James Tiptree, Jr.
THE DAYS OF PERKY PAT / THE MINORITY REPORT (1987)
{as Introduction}

K406. "Beyond the Enigma: Dick's Questors" by M.J. Tolley
      THE STELLAR GAUGE, Tolley/Sing, Norstrilia, 1980

K407. "The Collected Stories of Philip K. Dick" by M.J. Tolley
      Australian SF Review (fnz) #16, 9-88

K408. "Some Kinds of Life: An Account of Volume Two of THE
            COLLECTED STORIES OF PHILIP K. DICK: SECOND
            VARIETY" by Michael J. Tolley
      Australian SF Review (fnz) #24, Winter 1990

K409. Letter from Rev K.G. Trego (about Dick as a saint of the
            A-1 church of Eric Clapton)
      Surrealist Exchange ??

K410. "The First Annual Philip K. Dick Convention: Opening
            Address" by Paul C. Tumey
      The New York Review of SF (fnz) #70, 6-94

K411. "Blade Runner 2" by Kenneth Turan
      Los Angeles Times 1992
      Radio Free P.K.D. (fnz) #1, 2-93

K412. Letter to Bruce Gillespie by George Turner
      PHILIP K. DICK: ELECTRIC SHEPHERD, Gillespie,
            Norstrilia, 1975

K413. "NOW WAIT FOR LAST YEAR" by George Turner
      PHILIP K. DICK: ELECTRIC SHEPHERD, Gillespie,
            Norstrilia, 1975

K414. "Philip K. Dick by 1975: FLOW MY TEARS, THE POLICEMAN
            SAID" by George Turner
      PHILIP K. DICK: ELECTRIC SHEPHERD, Gillespie,
            Norstrilia, 1975

K415. "Philip K. Dick Saying it All Over Again" by
            George Turner
      PHILIP K. DICK: ELECTRIC SHEPHERD, Gillespie,
            Norstrilia, 1975

K416. "Philip K. Dick: A Bibliography" by M.B. Tymn
      PHILIP K. DICK, Greenberg/Olander, Taplinger, 1983

K417. "`Faith of Our Fathers': A Comparison of the Original
         Manuscript with the Published Text" by Sam
         Umland
       PKDS Newsletter (fnz) #29, 9-92

K418. "Regarding a 1964 letter to Tony Boucher" by Sam Umland
         [on G48]
       Radio Free P.K.D. (fnz) #2, 5-93

K419. "The Selected Letters Project" by Tim Underwood
       Radio Free P.K.D. (fnz) #4, 3-94

K420. "In Memoriam Philip K Dick 1928-1982" by Peter Viereck
       Isaac Asimov's SF Magazine 11-83

K421. "In the World He Was Writing About: The Life of Philip
         K. Dick" by Jeff Wagner
       Foundation #34, Autumn 1985

K422. "Who's Afraid of Philip K. Dick" by Paul Walker
       Science Fiction Review (fnz) #36, 3-70

K423. "Philip K. Dick: Exile in Paradox" by Eugene Warren
       Christianity Today 20-5-77

K424. "The Search for Absolutes" by Eugene Warren
       PHILIP K. DICK, Greenberg/Olander, Taplinger, 1983

K425. Entry by Patricia S. Warrick
       THE NEW ENCYCLOPEDIA OF SCIENCE FICTION, Gunn, Viking, 1988

K426. "The Encounter of Taoism and Fascism in THE MAN IN THE HIGH
         CASTLE" by Patricia S. Warrick
       Science Fiction Studies #21, 7-80
       PHILIP K. DICK, Greenberg/Olander, Taplinger, 1983
       ON PHILIP K. DICK, Mullen/Csicsery-Ronay/Evans/Hollinger,
         SF-TH Inc, 1992

K427. "In Memory of Philip K. Dick" by Patricia S. Warrick
       Science Fiction Studies #27, 7-82
       ON PHILIP K. DICK, Mullen/Csicsery-Ronay/Evans/Hollinger,
         SF-TH Inc, 1992

K428. "Into the Electronic Future" by Patricia S. Warrick
        THE CYBERNETIC IMAGINATION IN SCIENCE FICTION,
            Warrick, MIT Press, 1980

K429. "The Labyrinthian Process of the Artificial: Philip K Dick's
            Androids and Mechanical Constructs" by Patricia
            S. Warrick
        Extrapolation Vol 20 #2, Summer 1979
        SELECTED PROCEEDINGS OF THE 1978 SFRA NATIONAL CONFERENCE,
            University of North Iowa, 1979
        PHILIP K. DICK, Greenberg/Olander, Taplinger, 1983

K430. "Philip K. Dick's Answers to the Eternal Riddles" by
            Patricia S. Warrick
        THE TRANSCENDENT ADVENTURE, Reilly, Greenwood, 1984

K431. "The PKDS Interview with K.W. Jeter" by Andy Watson
        PKDS Newsletter (fnz) #5, 12-84

K432. "Le Guin's LATHE OF HEAVEN and the Role of Dick: The False
            Reality as Mediator" by Ian Watson
        Science-Fiction Studies #5, 3-75
        ON PHILIP K. DICK, Mullen/Csicsery-Ronay/Evans/Hollinger,
            SF-TH Inc, 1992

K433. "The Cult of Philip K. Dick" by Andrew Weiner
        REM (fnz) #6, 10-86

K434. "Resurrection from the Trash Heap" by Fay Weldon
        The Daily Telegraph 2-7-94

K435. Letter by Ted White (about Dick's "dark side")
        Science Fiction Review (fnz) #49, 11-83

K436. "The Author and the Oracle" by Paul Williams
        PKDS Newsletter (fnz) #25, 12-90

K437. "Confessions - The Press" by Paul Williams
        PKDS Newsletter (fnz) #29, 9-92

K438. Editorial Preface by Paul Williams
        THE SELECTED LETTERS OF PHILIP K. DICK: 1974 (1991)

K439. Foreword by Paul Williams
       THE MAN WHOSE TEETH WERE ALL EXACTLY ALIKE (1984)

K440. Introduction by Paul Williams
       CONFESSIONS OF A CRAP ARTIST (1975)

K441. Introduction by Paul Williams
       COSMOGONY AND COSMOLOGY (1987)

K442. Introduction by Paul Williams
       THE DARK-HAIRED GIRL (1988)

K443. Introduction by Paul Williams
       THE THREE STIGMATA OF PALMER ELDRITCH (1979)
       {Gregg Press edition only}

K444. Introduction by Paul Williams
       WELCOME TO REALITY, Anton, Broken Mirrors Press, 1991

K445. Introduction to `Fawn, Look Back' by Paul Williams
       Science Fiction Eye (fnz) #2, 8-87

K446. Introduction to `If You Find This World Bad, You Should
              See Some of the Others' by Paul Williams
       PKDS Newsletter (fnz) #27, 8-91

K447. Introduction to `Joe Protagoras is Alive and Well and
              Living on Earth' and `The Name of the Game is
              Death' by Paul Williams
       NEW WORLDS 2, Garnett, Gollancz, 1992

K448. Introduction to `Warning: We are Your Police' by Paul Williams
       PKDS Newsletter (fnz) #7, 7-85

K449. Introduction to WILKOMMEN IN DER WIRKLICHKEIT ("The
              Life-After-Life of Philip K. Dick") by
              Paul Williams
       PKDS Newsletter (fnz) #18, 8-88

K450. Introduction by Paul Williams
       UBIK: THE SCREENPLAY (1985)

K451. Letter by Paul Williams
       Locus (fnz) #272, 9-83

K452. "Media Stories about PKD, 1982 - An Incomplete Listing" by
       Paul Williams
       PKDS Newsletter (fnz) #1, 8-83

K453. "Media Stories about PKD, 1983 - An Incomplete Listing" by
       Paul Williams
       PKDS Newsletter (fnz) #2, 12-83

K454. "Philip K. Dick Appreciation" by Paul Williams
       Locus (fnz) #256, 5-82
       Science Fiction Chronicle (fnz) 5-82

K455. "Philip K. Dick's Romance with Germany" by Paul Williams
       privately circulated

K456. A PKD Chronology by Paul Williams
       IN PURSUIT OF VALIS: SELECTIONS FROM THE EXEGESIS (1991)

K457. "Reflections on Phil Dick" by Paul Williams [interview by
       John Fairchild]
       Radio Free P.K.D. (fnz) #1, 2-93 (part 1)
       Radio Free P.K.D. (fnz) #2, 5-93 (part 2)

K458. "The Rickmanization of PKD" by Paul Williams
       PKDS Newsletter (fnz) #24, 5-90 {as editorial}

K459. "Thrilling Wonder Stories" by Paul Williams [column on PKD]
       New York Avatar c. 1967/68
       ONLY APPARENTLY REAL, Williams, Arbor House, 1986 {extract}

K460. "THE THREE STIGMATA OF PALMER ELDRITCH" by Tad Williams
       HORROR: 100 BEST BOOKS, Jones/Newman, Xanadu, 1988

K461. "Afterwards" by Robert Anton Wilson
       PHILIP K. DICK: THE DREAM CONNECTION, Apel,
       Permanent Press, 1987

K462. "Fore-Words: PKD Deconstructed and Reconstructed" by Robert
       Anton Wilson
       THE SELECTED LETTERS OF PHILIP K. DICK: 1977-1979 (1993)

K463. "The Return of Philip K. Dick" by Robert Anton Wilson
      Magical Blend (fnz) #18, 2/3/4-88

K464. "Brahmin Awakening: Phil Dick & the Metaphysical Picaresque"
            by David Wingrove
      Vector (fnz) #85, 1/2-78

K465. "Understanding the Grasshopper: Leitmotifs and the Moral
            Dilemma in the Novels of Philip K. Dick" by
            David Wingrove
      Foundation #26, 10-82

K466. "Not Quite Coming to Terms" by Gary K. Wolfe [review of
            MIND IN MOTION: THE FICTION OF PHILIP K. DICK by
            Patricia S. Warrick]
      Science-Fiction Studies #45, 7-88
      ON PHILIP K. DICK, Mullen/Csicsery-Ronay/Evans/Hollinger,
            SF-TH Inc, 1992

K467. Entry by Anthony Wolk
      TWENTIETH-CENTURY SCIENCE-FICTION WRITERS, Smith,
            Macmillan, 1981

K468. "Philip K. Dick Appreciation" by Anthony Wolk
      Locus (fnz) #256, 5-82

K469. "The Sunstruck Forest: A Guide to the Short Fiction of
            Philip K. Dick" by Anthony Wolk
      Foundation #18, 1-80

K470. "Novelist Looked at Inner, Outer Space" by Paul Wong
      Los Angeles Times 9-3-82

K471. Introduction by Roger Zelazny
      BEYOND LIES THE WUB / THE SHORT HAPPY LIFE OF THE BROWN
            OXFORD (1987)

K472. "A Burnt-Out Case?" by Roger Zelazny
      Speech at Unicon, Australia, Easter 1978
      SF Commentary (fnz) #54, 11-78
      PKDS Newsletter (fnz) #16, 1-88 {condensed, as "Musings
            from Melbourne"}

K473. "Caught in the Movement of a Hand-Wound Universe" by
            Roger Zelazny
        PHILIP K. DICK: IN HIS OWN WORDS by Gregg Rickman,
            Fragments West, 1984 {as introduction}

K474. "Philip K. Dick Appreciation" by Roger Zelazny
        Locus (fnz) #256, 5-82

K475. "Philip K. Dick: Electric Shepherd by Roger Zelazny
        PHILIP K. DICK: ELECTRIC SHEPHERD, Gillespie,
            Norstrilia, 1975

K476. Entry by M.H. Zool
        THE BLOOMSBURY GOOD READING GUIDE TO SCIENCE FICTION

L. Reviews

   L1. THE BEST OF PHILIP K. DICK
        Booklist 1-6-77 (D. Miller)
        Chicago Daily News Panorama 28-5-77 (D. Miller)
        Cosmos 9-77 (Robert Silverberg)
        Fantasy and Science Fiction 8-78 (Barry N. Malzberg)
        Kliatt Paperback Guide Spring 1977 (E. Boatner)
        Library Journal 15-2-77 (B. Baker)
        Publishers Weekly 31-1-77
        SF&F Journal (fnz) #91, 5-81 (J. Goldfrank)

   L2. BEYOND LIES THE WUB
        FTL (fnz) #6, Autumn 1990 (John Kenny)
        Vector (fnz) #150, 6/7-89 (John Gribbin)

   L3. THE BOOK OF PHILIP K. DICK
        Kliatt Paperback Book Guide 4-73
        Luna Monthly (fnz) #46, 3-73 (L. Bloom)

L4. THE BROKEN BUBBLE
       Booklist 1-6-88
       Foundation #46, Autumn 1989 (Stef Lewicki)
       Kirkus Reviews 1-5-88
       Library Journal 15-6-88
       New York Times Book Review 16-10-88
       PKDS Newsletter (fnz) #17, 4-88 (Andy Watson)
       Publishers Weekly 27-5-88
       San Francisco Chronicle 29-6-88 (Michael Berry)
       Sunday Times 6-8-89 (Colin Greenland)
       Thrust (fnz) #31, Fall 1988 (Andrew Andrews)
       Times Literary Supplement 8-12-89 (John Clute)
       Venue 1-9-89 (Robin Askew)
       [see also K217]

L5. CLANS OF THE ALPHANE MOON
       Bookworld 27-4-80
       Bookworld 24-6-84
       The Daily Telegraph
       Fantasy Review (fnz) #71, 9-84 (Peter A. Brigg)
       Future Life #17, 3-80 (B. Mecoy)
       Kliatt Paperback Book Guide 4-72 (C. Richey)
       New York Times 11-5-80 (G. Jonas)
       Science Fiction Chronicle (fnz) 9-84 (Don D'Ammassa)
       SF Commentary (fnz) #1, 1-69 (Bruce Gillespie)
       Washington Post Book World 24-6-84 (C. Gardnner)

L6. THE COLLECTED STORIES OF PHILIP K. DICK
       The Independent 15-7-89 (David Barrett)
       PKDS Newsletter (fnz) #13, 2-87 (Andy Watson)
       SF & FANTASY BOOK REVIEW ANNUAL 1988 (R. Latham)
       Washington Post Book World 2-8-87 (David Streitfeld)

L7. CONFESSIONS OF A CRAP ARTIST
       Booklist 15-12-78
       Fiction #292, 7/8-78 (Roger Bozzetto)
       Janus (fnz) #14, Winter 1978/79 (Lee Carson)
       Library Journal 7-78 (D. Petticoffer)
       Locus (fnz) #177, 10-8-75 (Dick Lupoff)
       Locus (fnz) #180, 27-10-75 (Charles N. Brown)
       Publishers Weekly 17-4-78
       Vector (fnz) #96, 12-79/1-80 (Alan Dorey)

L8. THE COSMIC PUPPETS
       Astounding 6-58; 9-58 (UK); (P. Schuyler Miller)
       Fantasy and Science Fiction 1-58 (Anthony Boucher)
       Foundation #37, Autumn 1986 (Stef Lewicki)
       Punch 6-11-85
       Science Fiction Chronicle (fnz) 12-83 (Don D'Ammassa)
       SF Adventures 3-58 (Calvin Knox)

L9. COSMOGONY AND COSMOLOGY
   PKDS Newsletter (fnz) #16, 1-88 (Jonathan Lethem)

L10. COUNTER-CLOCK WORLD
   Fantasy and Science Fiction 11-67 (Judith Merril)
   Quarber Merkur (fnz) 10-67 (Franz Rottensteiner)
   SF Commentary (fnz) #4, 7-69 (Bruce Gillespie)

L11. THE CRACK IN SPACE
   Fantasy and Science Fiction 11-67 (J. Merril)
   Kliatt Paperback Guide 9-74 (E. Sisco)
   New Worlds #163, 6-66 (James Colvin)
   SF Commentary (fnz) #4, 7-69 (Bruce Gillespie)

L12. THE DARK-HAIRED GIRL
   Forced Exposure (fnz) #15, Summer 1989 (Jimmy Johnson)
   Forced Exposure (fnz) #16, 1990 (Lewis Shiner)
   New Pathways #14, 5-89 (Misha)
   PKDS Newsletter (fnz) #20, 4-89 (Jonathan Lethem)
   Thrust (fnz) #33, Spring 1989 (Andrew Andrews)
   Washington Post 26-3-89
   Weird Tales Fall 1989 (John Gregory Betancourt)

L13. DEUS IRAE
   Best Sellers 11-76 (R. Rafalko)
   Booklist 1-9-76 (D. Miller)
   Delap's F&SF Review (fnz) 2-77 (J. Sanders)
   Foundation #13, 5-78 (Tom Shippey)
   Galileo #6, 1-78 (R. Rouse)
   Publishers Weekly 5-7-76
   School Library Journal 3-77 (J. Daly)
   Science Fiction Review (fnz) #19, 8-76 (Richard E. Geis)
   Science Fiction Review Monthly (fnz) #20, 10-76 (N. Conan)
   SF Booklog (fnz) #12, 9-76 (Don D'Ammassa)
   Times Literary Supplement 8-7-77 (E. Korn)
   Unearth Winter 1977 (C. Gardner)
   Vector (fnz) #79, 1/2-77 (Chris Morgan)

L14. THE DIVINE INVASION
    Analog 7-12-81 (Tom Easton)
    Bestsellers 8-81
    Booklist 15-9-81 (R. Green)
    Books & Bookmen 8-82
    Bookworld 22-2-82
    Extrapolation Fall 1982 (Thomas D. Clareson)
    Interzone #2, Summer 1982 (Colin Greenland)
    Kirkus Reviews 1-4-81
    Kliatt Paperback Guide 1-83 (V. Livada)
    Library Journal 15-6-81 (S. Nickerson)
    Patchin Review (fnz) #2, 9-81
    Publishers Weekly 15-5-81
    Twilight Zone 9-82 (Thomas M. Disch)
    Vector (fnz) #104, 10-81 (Paul Kincaid)
    Village Voice Supplement 8-82
    [see also F41]

L15. DIVINE INVASIONS by Lawrence Sutin
    Chicago Tribune 20-2-90 (John Litweiler)
    Locus (fnz) #346, 11-89 (Tom Whitmore)
    Minneapolis Star Tribune 6-5-90 (Eric M. Heideman)
    New Scientist (David Barrett)
    Q (Andy Gill)
    Quantum (fnz) #37, Summer 1990 (Richard E. Geis)
    Science Fiction Review (fnz) #2, Summer 1990 (Andrew M. Andrews)
    USA Today (Gregory Feeley)
    Washington Post Book World 31-12-89 (Peter Nicholls)

L16. DO ANDROIDS DREAM OF ELECTRIC SHEEP?
    Analog 9-68 (P. Schuyler Miller)
    Books & Bookmen 6-69
    Cosmos (fnz) #2, 5-69 (Francis Arnold)
    Fantasy and Science Fiction 8-68 (J. Merril)
    FTL (fnz) #7, Winter 1990 (John Kenny)
    Kirkus Reviews 15-1-68
    Library Journal 1-3-68
    New Worlds #190, 5-69 (Harry Harrison)
    Publishers Weekly 29-1-68
    Science Fiction Review (fnz) #33, 10-69 (Richard E. Geis)
    SF Commentary (fnz) #7, 11-69 (D. Penman)
    SF Commentary (fnz) #9, 2-70 (Bruce Gillespie)
    Son of WSFA Journal (fnz) #26, 7-71 (S. Goldstein)
    Spectator 4-4-69
    The Sunday Times
    Times Literary Supplement 12-6-69
    Vector (fnz) #53, Spring/Summer 1969 (Gerald Bishop)
    Village Voice Supplement 8-82

L17. DR. BLOODMONEY
    Bookworld 28-4-85
    Kliatt Paperback Guide 9-76
    New Worlds #160, 3-66 (James Colvin)
    Science Fiction Studies 7-78 (R. Mullen)
    SF Commentary (fnz) #1, 1-69 (Bruce Gillespie)

L18. DR. FUTURITY
    Analog 10-60 (P. Schuyler Miller)
    Drilkjis (fnz) #2, 1976 (Kevin Smith)
    Fantasy and Science Fiction 6-60 (Damon Knight)
    If 7-60 (Frederik Pohl)
    Nexus (fnz) #2, 3/4-77 (David Wingrove)

L19. EYE IN THE SKY
    Astounding 1-58 (P. Schuyler Miller)
    Cypher (fnz) #6, 10/12-71 (Jim Goddard)
    Fantasy and Science Fiction 7-57 (Anthony Boucher)
    Infinity 11-57 (Damon Knight)
    L.A. Reader 15-12-89 (Steven Kane)
    Locus (fnz) #174, 3-6-75 (Charles N. Brown)
    New Statesman 20-8-71
    San Francisco Chronicle 22-9-57
    Science Fiction Review Monthly (fnz) #2, 4-75 (M. Last)
    Shark Tactics (fnz) 8-87 (Martyn Taylor)
    Venture 9-57 (Theodore Sturgeon)

L20. THE FATHER-THING
    Baltimore City Paper 4-91 (John Strausbaugh); reprinted
        in New York Press

L21. FLOW MY TEARS THE POLICEMAN SAID
    Algol (fnz) #22, 5-74 (Dick Lupoff)
    The Alien Critic (fnz) #9, 5-74 (Richard E. Geis)
    American Libraries 3-75
    Analog 12-74 (P. Schuyler Miller)
    Booklist 15-4-74
    Bookworld 26-7-81
    Delap's F&SF Review (fnz) #4, 7-75 (Cy Chauvin)
    Fantasy and Science Fiction 1-75 (Joanna Russ)
    Galaxy 8-74 (Theodore Sturgeon)
    Glass Keys (fnz) 6-78 (George Turner)
    Kirkus Reviews 1-12-73
    Library Journal 1-4-74
    The Listener 29-5-75
    Locus (fnz) #162, 20-7-74 (Peter Fitting)
    Locus (fnz) #166, 23-10-74 (Charles N. Brown)
    Locus (fnz) #174, 3-6-75 (Charles N. Brown)
    Luna Monthly (fnz) #51, Spring 1974 (Paul Walker)
    New Scientist 24-10-74 (N. Valery)

L21. FLOW MY TEARS THE POLICEMAN SAID (cont)
New York Times Book Review 20-7-75 (G. Jones)
The Observer 8-12-74
Psychology Today 6-74
Publishers Weekly 3-12-73
Science Fiction Review Monthly (fnz) #2, 4-75 (David Hartwell)
SF Commentary (fnz) #41/42, 2-75 (Barry Gillam)
SF Monthly 12-74 (Malcolm Edwards)
Son of WSFA Journal (fnz) #185/186, 5-75 (Don D'Ammassa)
Vector (fnz) #78, 11/12-76 (David Wingrove)
Vertex 10-74

L22. FLOW MY TEARS, THE POLICEMAN SAID (play)
Newsweek 4-7-88
The New York Times 18-6-88 (Mel Gussow)
The Village Voice 28-6-88 (J. Hoberman)

L23. GALACTIC POT-HEALER
Analog 3-70 (P. Schuyler Miller)
Books and Bookmen 10-71 (D. Compton)
The Evening Standard
Kliatt Paperback Guide 9-74
Luna Monthly (fnz) #13, 6-70 (S. Mines)
Lurk (fnz) #5, 10-73 (Phil Payne)
New Worlds #194, 10-69 (Joyce Churchill)
The Observer 21-11-71
Publishers Weekly 5-5-69
Science Fiction Review (fnz) #35, 2-70 (Mats Linder)
The Scotsman
Vector (fnz) #55, 1970
WSFA Journal (fnz) #73, 9/11-70 (Alexis Gilliland)
Zimri (fnz) #4½, 1973 (Chris Morgan)

L24. THE GAME-PLAYERS OF TITAN
Amazing 5-64 (Robert Silverberg)
Analog 8-64 (P. Schuyler Miller)
Fiction #294, 10-78 (Roger Bozzetto)
Kliatt Paperback Book Guide 9-72 (C. Richey)
Vector (fnz) #83, 10-77 (Andrew Darlington)

L25. THE GANYMEDE TAKEOVER
New Worlds #176, 10-67 (James Cawthorn)
SF Commentary (fnz) #2, 3-69 (Bruce Gillespie)

L26. THE GOLDEN MAN
     Analog 8-80 (Spider Robinson)
     Fantasy and Science Fiction 7-80 (Thomas M. Disch)
     Galaxy 7-80 (A. Ryan)
     Quarber Merkur (fnz) 7-81
     Science Fiction (fnz) 9-81 (Terry Dowling)
     Vector (fnz) #105, 12-81 (David Penn)

L27. A HANDFUL OF DARKNESS
     Authentic #62, 10-55 (H.J. Campbell)
     British Space Fiction 10-55
     Fantasy and Science Fiction 4-56 (Anthony Boucher)
     New Worlds #40, 10-55 (Leslie Flood)
     Science Fiction Review (fnz) #32, 8-79 (Tom Staicar)

L28. HUMPTY DUMPTY IN OAKLAND
     Foundation #39, Spring 1987 (Ian Watson)
     The London Review of Books 5-2-87
     The Observer 19-10-86
     PKDS Newsletter (fnz) #13, 2-87 (Andy Watson)
     Times Literary Supplement 6-2-87 (John Clute)
     Vector (fnz) #137, 4/5-87 (Paul Kincaid)

L29. I HOPE I SHALL ARRIVE SOON
     Booklist 15-9-85
     Bookworld 30-6-85
     Fantasy Review (fnz) 7-85
     Interzone #16, Summer 1986 (Alex Stewart)
     Publishers Weekly 3-5-85
     Publishers Weekly 21-8-87
     San Francisco Chronicle 10-85
     Science Fiction Review (fnz) #60, 8-86 (Andrew Andrews)
     SF Spectrum (fnz) #1, 1986 (Steve Sneyd)
     Times Literary Supplement 7-2-86 (Colin Greenland)
     Voice of Youth Advocates 12-85

L30. IN MILTON LUMKY TERRITORY
     Books & Bookmen 1-86
     Foundation #37, Autumn 1986 (Stef Lewicki)
     New Musical Express 11-4-87 (D.J. Fontana)
     The Observer 3-11-85
     PKDS Newsletter (fnz) #11, 5-86 (Andy Watson)
     Publishers Weekly 31-5-85
     Thrust (fnz) #23, Fall/Winter 1985 (Michael Bishop)
     Times Literary Supplement 17-1-86 (John Clute)
     [see also K361]

L31. IN PURSUIT OF VALIS: SELECTIONS FROM THE EXEGESIS
    Locus (fnz) #374, 3-92 (Dan Chow)
    Science Fiction Eye (fnz) #10, 6-92 (John Shirley)
    Trajectories (fnz) Autumn 1991 (Robert Anton Wilson)
    [see also K329]

L32. THE LITTLE BLACK BOX
    Interzone #47, 5-91 (Ken Brown)

L33. THE MAN IN THE HIGH CASTLE
    Amazing 2-63 (S.E. Cotts)
    Amazing 6-64 (Robert Silverberg)
    Analog 4-63 (P. Schuyler Miller)
    Books 7-88
    Commonweal 1-8-75
    Fantasy and Science Fiction 6-63 (Avram Davidson)
    Kliatt Paperback Guide 9-74
    Koinos Kosmos (fnz) 6-82 (Terence M. Green)
    Library Journal 15-11-88
    The Listener 29-5-75
    Locus (fnz) #174, 3-6-75 (Charles N. Brown)
    New Musical Express 11-4-87 (D.J. Fontana)
    New Statesman 24-4-87
    New Worlds #160, 3-66 (James Colvin)
    New Worlds #173, 7-67 (James Cawthorn)
    The Observer 8-6-75
    Science Fiction Studies 7-88
    SF Commentary (fnz) #1, 1-69 (Bruce Gillespie)
    SF Commentary (fnz) #47, 8-76 (Terence M. Green)
    SF Monthly Vol 3 #1, 1-76 (Malcolm Edwards)
    Son of WSFA Journal (fnz) #151/152, 6-74 (D. Stever)
    Times Literary Supplement 23-5-75
    Vector (fnz) #138, 6/7-87 (Jim England)

L34. THE MAN WHO JAPED
    Astounding 8-57; 12-57 (UK); (P. Schuyler Miller)
    Fantastic 5-57 (Villiers Gerson)
    Fantasy and Science Fiction 4-57 (Anthony Boucher)
    Infinity 4-57 (Larry T. Shaw & Irwin Stein)
    Locus (fnz) #170, 15-3-75 (Tom Whitmore)

L35. THE MAN WHOSE TEETH WERE ALL EXACTLY ALIKE
     Bookworld 29-7-84
     Fantasy Review (fnz) #73, 11-84 (Ed Burns)
     Interzone #9, Autumn 1984 (David Pringle)
     Locus (fnz) #283, 8-84 (Dan Chow)
     New Musical Express 25-10-86 (D.J. Fontana)
     PKDS Newsletter (fnz) #11, 5-86 (Andy Watson)
     San Francisco Chronicle 2-85
     Science Fiction Review (fnz) #52, 8-84 (Richard E. Geis)
     Thrust (fnz) #21, Fall 1984/Winter 1985 (Ed Burns)
     Thrust (fnz) #23, Fall/Winter 1985 (Michael Bishop)
     Twilight Zone 11/12-84 (Thomas M. Disch)
     Vector (fnz) #137, 4/5-87 (Paul Kincaid)
     Washington Post Book World 29-7-84 (Charles Platt)

L36. MARTIAN TIME-SLIP
     Analog 11-64 (P. Schuyler Miller)
     Bookworld 26-7-81
     Fantasy and Science Fiction 12-64 (Ron Goulart)
     New Statesman 17-12-76 (J.G. Ballard)
     The Observer 8-8-76
     Patchin Review (fnz) #1, 7-81
     SF Commentary (fnz) #48/49/50, 10/12-76
             (Bruce Gillespie)

L37. MARY AND THE GIANT
     Bookworld 2-8-87
     Kirkus Reviews 1-3-87
     Library Journal 15-5-87
     New York Times Book Review 26-4-87
     PKDS Newsletter (fnz) #15, 8-87 (Andy Watson)
     Publishers Weekly 20-3-87
     Times Literary Supplement 19-2-88 (Colin Greenland)
     Washington Post Book World 2-8-87 (David Streitfeld)

L38. A MAZE OF DEATH
     Books and Bookmen 3-72 (B. Patten)
     Kirkus Reviews 15-5-70
     Kliatt Paperback Book Guide 2-72 (C. Richey)
     Library Journal 15-11-70 (M. Blalock)
     Luna Monthly (fnz) #26/27, 7/8-71 (D. Paskow)
     The Observer 5-3-72
     Publishers Weekly 11-5-70
     Punch 6-3-85
     Science Fiction Review (fnz) #39, 8-70 (Richard E. Geis)
     Science Fiction Review (fnz) #48, 8-83 (Richard E. Geis)
     Son of WSFA Journal (fnz) #25, 6-71 (J. Newton)
     Speculation (fnz) #29, 10-71 (Philip Strick)
     The Sunday Times

L39. MIND IN MOTION: THE FICTION OF PHILIP K. DICK by
        Patricia S. Warrick
     PKDS Newsletter (fnz) #16, 1-88 (Jonathan Lethem)
     [see also K466]

L40. NICK AND THE GLIMMUNG
     Foundation #46, Autumn 1989 (Nicholas Hyman)
     PKDS Newsletter (fnz) #18, 8-88 (Andy Watson)
     Times Literary Supplement 30-9-88 (Linda Taylor)

L41. NOW WAIT FOR LAST YEAR
     Library Journal 1-5-66
     Locus (fnz) #162, 20-7-74 (Charles N. Brown)
     The New Yorker 27-1-75
     Patchin Review (fnz) #3, 1-82
     SF Commentary (fnz) #9, 2-70 (Bruce Gillespie)
     SF Commentary (fnz) #9, 2-70 (George Turner)

L42. ONLY APPARENTLY REAL by Paul Williams
     PKDS Newsletter (fnz) #11, 5-86 (Andy Watson)
     Science Fiction Eye (fnz) #2, 8-87 (Ted White)
     Science Fiction Review (fnz) #60, 8-86 (Gene DeWeese)
     [see also K153]

L43. ON PHILIP K. DICK edited by R.D. Mullen et al.
     Foundation #58, Summer 1993 (Robert Irwin)

L44. OUR FRIENDS FROM FROLIX 8
     Luna Monthly (fnz) #24/25, 5/6-71 (J. Evers)
     Vector (fnz) #72, 2-76 (Christopher Evans)
     [see also K217]

L45. THE PENULTIMATE TRUTH
     American Book Review 1-85
     Amazing 4-65 (Robert Silverberg)
     Bookworld 27-4-80
     Christian Science Monitor 20-6-84
     Fantasy Review (fnz) #69, 7-84 (Peter Brigg)
     Future Life #17, 3-80 (B. Mecoy)
     Kliatt Paperback Guide 4-80 (M. Loo)
     The Observer 24-9-67
     Punch 2-8-67
     Science Fiction Chronicle (fnz) 9-84 (Don D'Ammassa)
     Science Fiction Review Monthly (fnz) #10, 12-75 (L. Knapp)
     SF Commentary (fnz) #2, 3-70 (Bruce Gillespie)
     The Sunday Times 6-8-67 (Edmund Cooper)
     Times Literary Supplement 29-6-67
     Voice of Youth Advocates 2-85

L46. PHILIP K. DICK by Douglas A. Mackey
      Foundation #44, Winter 1987/88 (Stef Lewicki)
      PKDS Newsletter (fnz) #18, 8-88 (Gregg Rickman)
      [see also K147]

L47. PHILIP K. DICK edited by Joseph D. Olander & Martin H.
           Greenberg
      Locus (fnz) #268, 5-83 (Dan Chow)
      Los Angeles Times 5-6-83 (Chris Wall)
      PKDS Newsletter (fnz) #2, 12-83 (Frank C. Bertrand)

L48. PHILIP K. DICK: ELECTRIC SHEPHERD edited by Bruce Gillespie
      Foundation #10, 6-76

L49. PHILIP K. DICK: IN HIS OWN WORDS by Gregg Rickman
      Analog 5-85
      Booklist 15-1-85
      Fantasy and Science Fiction 3-86 (Algis Budrys)
      Fantasy Review (fnz) 1-85
      Niekas (fnz) #33, 1985 (Edmund R. Meskys)
      Publishers Weekly 14-9-84
      San Francisco Chronicle 5-85
      Science Fiction Review (fnz) #53, 11-84 (Richard E. Geis)
      Thrust (fnz) #35, Winter 1990 (Andrew Andrews)

L50. A PHILIP K. DICK OMNIBUS
      Cypher (fnz) #3, 12-70 (R. Waddington)
      The Sunday Times 10-1-71 (Edmund Cooper)

L51. PHILIP K. DICK: THE DREAM CONNECTION edited by D. Scott Apel
      PKDS Newsletter (fnz) #15, 8-87 (Andy Watson)

L52. PHILIP K. DICK: THE LAST TESTAMENT by Gregg Rickman
      Fantasy and Science Fiction 3-86 (Algis Budrys)

L53. PKD: A BIBLIOGRAPHY by Daniel H. Levack & Steven Owen Godersky
      Chicago magazine ? (David Standish)
      Heavy Metal 7-82 (?) (Tomothy Lucas)
      [see also K153]

L54. THE PRESERVING MACHINE
      Books & Bookmen 5-71
      Cypher (fnz) #4, 4-71 (Jim Goddard)
      The Daily Telegraph
      The Evening Standard
      Luna Monthly (fnz) #9, 2-70 (J. Slavin)
      Lurk (fnz) #5, 10-73 (Phil Payne)
      New Musical Express 28-11-87 (Richard North)
      Science Fiction Review (fnz) #34, 12-69 (Richard Delap)
      SF&F Newsletter (fnz) #10, 9-76 (M. Wooster)
      Son of WSFA Journal (fnz) #17, 3-71 (yngvi)
      The Sunday Times 7-3-71 (Edmund Cooper)
      Times Literary Supplement 16-4-71
      Zimri (fnz) #4½, 1973 (Chris Morgan)

L55. PUTTERING ABOUT IN A SMALL LAND
      Analog 7-86
      Booklist 1-9-85
      Fantasy Review (fnz) 2-86
      Kirkus Reviews 15-9-85
      Los Angeles Times Book Review 9-2-86
      New Statesman 9-10-87
      New York Times Book Review 1-12-85
      PKDS Newsletter (fnz) #11, 5-86 (Andy Watson)
      Publishers Weekly 4-10-85
      San Francisco Chronicle 8-12-85 (John Stanley)
      Saturday Review 2-86 (SR)
      USA Today 8-1-86

L56. RADIO FREE ALBEMUTH
      Booklist 1-12-85
      Bookworld 25-5-86
      Fantasy Review (fnz) 11-85
      Kirkus Reviews 15-11-85
      Library Journal 12-85
      New York Times 12-1-86 (Gerald Jonas)
      PKDS Newsletter (fnz) #11, 5-86 (Andy Watson)
      Publishers Weekly 1-11-85
      San Francisco Chronicle 5-86
      Saturday Review 2-86 (SR)
      Science Fiction Review (fnz) #60, 8-86 (Darrell Schweitzer)
      Thrust (fnz) #30, Summer 1988 (Andrew Andrews)
      Vector (fnz) #139, 8/9-87 (L. J. Hurst)

L57. RETROFITTING BLADE RUNNER by Judith P. Kerman
      Foundation #55, Summer 1992 (Stef Lewicki)
      [see also K200]

L58. ROBOTS, ANDROIDS AND MECHANICAL ODDITIES
Booklist 15-9-84 (R. Green)
Choice 11-84
Fantasy Review (fnz) #72, 10-84 (Paul Lloyd)
Foundation #32, 11-84 (John Clute)
Kliatt Young Adult Paperback Book Guide Fall 1986
Journal of American Studies 12-85
Locus (fnz) #283, 8-84 (Dan Chow)
North American Review 3-87
PKDS Newsletter (fnz) #11, 5-86 (Andy Watson)
Science Fiction Review (fnz) #60, 8-86 (Andrew Andrews)
Times Literary Supplement 18-1-85 (Thomas M. Disch)

L59. A SCANNER DARKLY
Best Sellers 5-77 (R. Hussain)
Booklist 1-3-77 (D. Miller)
Chicago Daily News Panorama 26-2-77 (D. Miller)
Cosmos 9-77 (Robert Silverberg)
Delap's F&SF Review (fnz) 2-78 (Michael Bishop)
Foundation #13, 5-78 (Brian Stableford)
Galaxy 8-77 (Spider Robinson)
Galileo #3, 4-77 (F. Kemske)
Kirkus Reviews 1-12-76
Kliatt Paperback Guide -78 (E. Boatner)
New Republic 26-11-77
New Statesman 16-12-77
The Observer 1-1-78
Publishers Weekly 15-11-76
Science Fiction Review (fnz) #20, 2-77 (Richard E. Geis)
Spectator 19-11-77
Times Literary Supplement 27-1-78 (Peter Parrinder)
Unearth Spring 1977 (T. Green)
Vector (fnz) #84, 11/12-77 (David Wingrove)

L60. SECOND VARIETY
Foundation #46, Autumn 1989 (Nicholas Hyman)
FTL (fnz) #7, Winter 1990

L61. THE SELECTED LETTERS OF PHILIP K. DICK: 1974
[see K329]

L62. SOLAR LOTTERY / WORLD OF CHANCE
     Astounding 11-55; 5-56 (UK); (P. Schuyler Miller)
     Astounding 8-56 (UK)
     Authentic #73, 9-56
     Cosmos 9-77 (Robert Silverberg)
     Cypher (fnz) #7, 5-72 (Martin Ricketts)
     Fantasy and Science Fiction 8-55 (Anthony Boucher)
     Galaxy 11-55 (Floyd C. Gale)
     Infinity 11-55 (Damon Knight)
     Isaac Asimov's SF Magazine Summer 1977 (Charles N. Brown)
     Kliatt Paperback Guide 2-76 (K. Reeds)
     Locus (fnz) #180, 27-10-75 (Charles N. Brown)
     New Worlds #49, 7-56 (Leslie Flood)
     New Worlds #184, 11-68 (R. Meadley & M. Harrison)
     Science Fiction Review (fnz) #22, 8-77 (Darrell Schweitzer)
     Science Fiction Review Monthly (fnz) #19, 9-76 (R. Klorese)
     Science Fiction Studies 11-76 (R. Mullen)
     Shark Tactics (fnz) 8-87 (Martyn Taylor)

L63. THE THREE STIGMATA OF PALMER ELDRITCH
     Analog 8-65 (P. Schuyler Miller)
     Books & Bookmen 9-66
     The Daily Telegraph
     Fantasy and Science Fiction 6-65 (Judith Merril)
     Galaxy 8-65 (A.J. Budrys); reprinted in BENCHMARKS, Budrys,
          Southern Illinois University Press, 1985
     Guardian Weekly 7-4-66
     National Review 9-3-65
     New Worlds #160, 3-66 (James Colvin)
     The Observer 3-4-66
     Punch 9-3-66
     Science Fiction Review Monthly (fnz) #5, 7-75 (N. Conan)
     SF Commentary (fnz) #1, 1-69 (Bruce Gillespie)
     Son of WSFA Journal (fnz) #68, 9-72 (Michael Shoemaker)
     Times Literary Supplement 24-3-66
     Vector (fnz) #40, 6-66 (Christopher Priest)
     Washington Post Book World 27-3-83

L64. TIME OUT OF JOINT
     Analog 1-60 (P. Schuyler Miller)
     Bookworld 27-4-80
     Bookworld 28-10-84
     Emergency Librarian 1-88
     Fantasy Review (fnz) 2-85
     Future Life #17, 3-80 (B. Mecoy)
     If 11-59 (Frederik Pohl)
     Kipple (fnz) #1, 2-77 (David Wingrove)
     Kliatt Young Adult Paperback Book Guide Winter 1985
     Punch 21-11-84

L65. TOTAL RECALL by Piers Anthony
     Foundation #51, Spring 1991 (Sherry Coldsmith)
     Interzone #40, 10-90 (Betka Wight)
     Science Fiction Chronicle (fnz) 9-89 (Don D'Ammassa)

L66. TO THE HIGH CASTLE: PHILIP K. DICK: A LIFE by Gregg Rickman
     Choice 3-90 (B. Kalikoff)
     Locus (fnz) #342, 7-89
     USA Today (Gregory Feeley)
     Washington Post Book World 31-12-89 (Peter Nicholls)
     [see also K153]

L67. THE TRANSMIGRATION OF TIMOTHY ARCHER
     American Book Review 9-83
     Analog 10-82 (Tom Easton)
     Best Sellers 8-82 (G. Mercurio)
     Bookworld 23-5-82
     Brigante (fnz) #4, 1985 (Eunice Pearson)
     Fantasy Newsletter (fnz) #51, 9-82 (Frank A. Smith)
     Foundation #26, 10-82 (Colin Greenland)
     Heavy Metal 7-82 (?) (Jay Kinney)
     Interzone #4, Spring 1983 (John Clute)
     Kirkus Reviews 15-3-82
     Library Journal 15-3-82
     Locus (fnz) #256, 5-82 (Debbie Notkin)
     Los Angeles Times 12-6-83 (Don Strachan)
     Nation 24-12-83
     Patchin Review (fnz) #6, 3/5-83
     Publishers Weekly 26-3-82
     San Francisco Chronicle 26-9-82 (Elizabeth A. Lynn)
     Science Fiction Chronicle (fnz) 7-83 (Don D'Ammassa)
     SF&F Book Review (fnz) #5, 6-82 (R. Reilly)
     Thrust (fnz) #19, Winter/Spring 1983 (Doug Fratz)
     Twilight Zone 9-82 (Thomas M. Disch)
     Vector (fnz) #112, -83 (Paul Kincaid)
     Village Voice Literary Supplement 8-82
     Wall Street Journal 8-7-82
     Washington Post Book World 23-5-82 (Robert Silverberg);
             PKDS Newsletter (fnz) #1, 8-83 {extract};
     West Coast Review of Books 11-82
     [see also K383]

L68. UBIK
    Amazing 3-84 (F. Catalano)
    Analog 10-69 (P. Schuyler Miller)
    Booklist 1-10-69
    The Evening Standard
    Kirkus Reviews 1-3-69
    Kliatt Young Adult Paperback Book Guide Spring 1977 (E. Boatner)
    Library Journal 15-12-69
    Luna Monthly (fnz) #4, 9-69 (S. Mines)
    The Observer 5-7-70
    Publishers Weekly 10-3-69
    Science Fiction Review (fnz) #32, 8-69 (Richard E. Geis)
    Science Fiction Review (fnz) #39, 8-70 (Richard E. Geis)
    SF Commentary (fnz) #9, 2-70 (Bruce Gillespie)
    SF Commentary (fnz) #17, 11-70 (George Turner)
    Speculation (fnz) #29, 10-71 (Philip Strick)
    The Sunday Times 8-70 (Edmund Cooper)
    Times Literary Supplement 9-7-70
    Venture 11-69 (Ron Goulart)
    WSFA Journal (fnz) #70, 12-69/2-70 (T. Pauls)

L69. UBIK: THE SCREENPLAY
    Fantasy Review (fnz) 10-85
    PKDS Newsletter (fnz) #11, 5-86
    San Francisco Chronicle 2-85

L70. THE UNTELEPORTED MAN / LIES, INC.
    Ad Astra #9, 1979
    Bookworld 31-7-83
    Drilkjis (fnz) #2, 1976 (Kevin Smith)
    Locus (fnz) #283, 8-84 (Dan Chow)
    Nexus (fnz) #2, 3/4-77 (David Wingrove)
    Publishers Weekly 10-6-83
    SF&F Book Review (fnz) #20, 12-83 (S. Lehman)
    Times Literary Supplement 18-1-85 (Thomas M. Disch)
    Washington Post Book World 31-7-83 (Somtow Sucharitkul)

L71. VALIS
    Analog 27-4-81 (Tom Easton)
    Books & Bookmen 8-82
    Bookworld 22-2-81
    Chicago magazine ? (David Standish)
    Commonweal 22-5-81
    Crystal Ship (fnz) #5, 1-82 (Iain Ewing)
    Fantasy and Science Fiction 7-81 (Thomas M. Disch)
    Fantasy and Science Fiction 8-81 (Algis J. Budrys)
    Foundation #22, 6-81 (Michael Bishop)
    Isaac Asimov's SF Magazine 16-3-81 (Baird Searles)
    Library Journal 15-2-81 (R. Herbert)
    PKDS Newsletter (fnz) #17, 4-88 (Andy Watson)
    Publishers Weekly 12-12-80

L71. VALIS (cont)
     Questar 6-81 (C. Henderson)
     SF Commentary (fnz) #62/63/64/65/66, 6-81 (Bruce Gillespie)
     Vector (fnz) #102, 6-81 (Paul Kincaid)
     Village Voice 15-4-81

L72. THE VALIS TRILOGY
     Austin Chronicle 30-8-91 (Ed Ward)

L73. THE VARIABLE MAN
     Analog 2-77 (Lester Del Rey)
     Astounding 9-58 (P. Schuyler Miller)
     Fantastic Universe 4-58 (Hans Stefan Santesson)
     Fantasy and Science Fiction 2-58 (Anthony Boucher)
     SF Adventures 6-58 (Calvin Knox)
     Vector (fnz) #83, 10-77 (Andrew Darlington)
     Venture 5-58 (Theodore Sturgeon)

L74. VULCAN'S HAMMER
     Amazing 2-61
     Analog 11-61 (P. Schuyler Miller)
     Nexus (fnz) #2, 3/4-77 (David Wingrove)

L75. WE CAN BUILD YOU
     Galaxy 1-73 (Theodore Sturgeon)
     Locus (fnz) #174, 3-6-75 (Charles N. Brown)
     Vector (fnz) #83, 10-77 (Andrew Darlington)

L76. WELCOME TO REALITY edited by Uwe Anton
     Science Fiction Eye (fnz) #9, 11-91 (Misha)

L77. THE WORLD JONES MADE
     Astounding 9-56 (P. Schuyler Miller)
     Delap's F&SF Review (fnz) 6-76 (A. Rothstein)
     Fantasy and Science Fiction 8-56 (Anthony Boucher)
     Infinity 10-56 (Damon Knight)
     New Worlds #187, 2-69 (James Cawthorn)
     Science Fiction Review Monthly (fnz) #12, 2-76 (W. MacPherson)
     SF Commentary (fnz) #2, 3-69 (Bruce Gillespie)
     Vector (fnz) #52, Winter/Spring 1969 (Bryn Fortey)
     Visions of Tomorrow 3-70 (Donald Malcolm)

L78. THE ZAP GUN
     Bookworld 28-4-83
     Fantasy and Science Fiction 11-67 (Judith Merril)
     Kirkus Reviews 1-1-85
     Psychotic (fnz) #21, 11-67 (Richard E. Geis)
     SF Commentary (fnz) #4, 7-69 (Bruce Gillespie)

M1. ENTROPIE UND HOFFNUNG by Uwe Anton
      Verlag Thomas Tilsner   , 1993? {in German}

M2. PHILIP K. DICK: THE DREAM CONNECTION edited by D. Scott Apel
         [K48, K49, G15, A33, G63, K283, K50, K461,
         G46, K381, G71]
      Permanent Press (hb)   , 3-87, 296pp, $19.95 (?)
         {limited to 500 copies}

M3. THE MEDIA NOVELS OF PHILIP K. DICK: CAUTIONARY FABLES FOR AN
         ELECTRONIC AGE by Heather Ashby
      Thesis, University of Guelph, 1987

M4. REALITY, RELIGION, AND POLITICS IN PHILIP K. DICK'S FICTION
         by Aaron J. Barlow
      Ph.D. Dissertation, University of Iowa, 1988

M5. THE SPLINTERED SHARDS: REALITY AND ILLUSION IN THE NOVELS OF
         PHILIP K. DICK by Claudia Krenz Bush
         [shortened version published as K227]
      Master's Thesis, Idaho State University, -75, 112pp

M6. JE SUIS VIVANT ET VOUS ÊTES MORTS by Emmanuel Carrère
      Unknown French publisher, 1993 {biography, in French}

M7. PHILIP K. DICK: ELECTRIC SHEPHERD by Bruce Gillespie
         [K475, K170, K171, K169, K173, K413, K415,
         G34, F2, K246, K414, G55, F22, K412, K295]
      Norstrilia Press (tp) 00-2, -75, 106pp, $A4.00 (Irene Pagram)
         {limited to 2000 copies}

M8. PHILIP K. DICK edited by Martin H. Greenberg & Joseph D.
         Olander [F17, K265, K150, K387, K41, K426, K64,
         K429, K424, K123, K190, K300, K416]
      Taplinger (hb) 6292-9, 5-83, 256pp, $12.95
      Taplinger (tp) 6291-0, 5-83, 256pp, $5.95

M9. RETROFITTING BLADE RUNNER: ISSUES IN RIDLEY SCOTT'S BLADE
         RUNNER AND PHILIP K. DICK'S DO ANDROIDS DREAM OF
         ELECTRIC SHEEP? by Judith Kerman [exp from K216]
      Bowling Green University (hb)   , -91, 291pp, $39.95
      Bowling Green University (tp)   , -91, 291pp, $19.95

M10. PKD: A PHILIP K. DICK BIBLIOGRAPHY by Daniel H. Levack &
        Steven Owen Godersky [incl G56 & G73]
        Underwood-Miller (hb) 34-X, 10-81, 158pp, $20.00 {limited
            to 233 copies, signed by Dick, Levack & Godersky}
        Underwood-Miller (hb) 34-X, 10-81, 158pp, $16.95 {limited
            to 326 copies}
        Underwood-Miller (tp) 33-1, 10-81, 158pp, $7.95
        Meckler (hb) 096-3, 9-88, 156pp, $45.00 (?) {minor
            corrections}

M11. PHILIP K. DICK by Douglas A. Mackey
        Twayne (hb) 7515-3, 3-88, 157pp, $19.95 (?)

M12. THE OEDIPUS MYTH IN TWENTIETH-CENTURY FICTION by
        D.A. Moddelmog
        Ph.D. Dissertation, Pennsylvania State Univeristy, 1985

M13. ON PHILIP K. DICK: 40 ARTICLES FROM SCIENCE-FICTION STUDIES
        edited by R.D. Mullen, Istvan Csicsery-Ronay, Jr.,
        Arthur B. Evans and Veronica Hollinger [C-43: K98,
        K269, K388, K387, G35, K289, K203, K41, K150, K244,
        K432, F5, K426, K427, K148, K155, K139, K35, K338,
        K357, K36, K146, K145, K154, K73, K151, K195, K321,
        K131, K356, K334, K206, K56, K466, K130, K147,
        K298, K153, K326, K292, K329, K200]
        SF-TH Inc (hb) 0-7, -92, 290pp
        SF-TH Inc (tp) 1-5, -92, 290pp

M14. PHILIP K. DICK by Hazel Pierce
        Starmont (tp) 33-9, 1-83, 64pp, $4.95 (?); ?, $7.95 (?);
        Starmont (hb) 34-7, 1-83, 64pp, $10.95 (?)
        Borgo (hb) 043-6, -83, 64pp, $10.95 (?); ?, $16.95 (?);

M15. PHILIP K. DICK: IN HIS OWN WORDS by Gregg Rickman
        [incl K473, K332, K330]
        Fragments West (tp) 01-1, 8-84, 250pp, $9.95 (?);
            -88, $9.95 {slightly revised};

M16. PHILIP K. DICK: THE LAST TESTAMENT by Gregg Rickman
        [incl G28, G71, K219, K351]
        Fragments West (tp) 02-X, 4-85, 238pp, $9.95 (?)

M17. TO THE HIGH CASTLE: PHILIP K. DICK: A LIFE 1928 - 1962
        by Gregg Rickman [incl A83, A109, A115, D2, N31,
        D8, D9, D10, G11, G33]
        Fragments West (tp) 24-0, 5-89, 451pp, $19.95 (?)

M18. THE NOVELS OF PHILIP K. DICK by Kim Stanley Robinson
     Ph.D. Dissertation, University of California, San Diego,
          -82, 251pp
     UMI Research (hb) 1589-2, -84, 150pp, $24.95 (?)
     UMI Research (tp)   , -91, 150pp, $19.95 (?)

M19. A CHECKLIST OF PHILIP K. DICK by Christopher P. Stephens
     Ultramarine (ph) 174-0, -90, 46pp   ; -91 {revised};

M20. DIVINE INVASIONS: A LIFE OF PHILIP K. DICK by Lawrence Sutin
          [incl A28 & D8]
     Harmony (hb) 57204-4, 12-89, 340pp, $25.95 (Rich Tassone)
     Citadel (tp) 1228-8, 6-91, 352pp, $12.95 (?)
     Paladin (tp) 09086-X, 11-91, 352pp, £8.99 (Frank Ronan)
     HarperCollins UK (tp) 21490-9, 2-94, 352pp, £8.99 (Ronan)

M21. PHILIP K. DICK & THE UMBRELLA OF LIGHT by Angus Taylor
     T.K. Graphics (tp)   , -75, 52pp, $2.25 (?)

M22. MIND IN MOTION: THE FICTION OF PHILIP K. DICK by
          Patricia S. Warrick
     Southern Illinois University Press (hb) 1326-X, 7-87,
          222pp, $18.95 (?)

M23. ONLY APPARENTLY REAL by Paul Williams [based on G32; incl
          ext from K459]
     Arbor House (hb) 800-9, 5-86, 184pp, $7.95 (G.K. Bellows)

M24. PHILIP K. DICK: A SECONDARY BIBLIOGRAPHY by H. Stephen Wright
     Privately published (ph)   , -88, 28pp, $7.00

M25. Bladerunner Special
     Fanzine published in 1993 (and reprinted in 1994) by Tony Lee
     to commemorate the 10th anniversary of the film's release.

M26. Denebola #9, 1-90 [incl O18, O24, O13]
     Special Philip K. Dick issue of a German fanzine.

M27. Foundation #26, 10-82 [K288, K43, K380, K465, K84, L67]
     Special Philip K. Dick section in the English critical
     magazine.

M28. Galaktika #52 [A134, A112, A94, A24, A1, A101, A9, A77, K233]
This issue, in 1983, of a popular Hungarian SF anthology/
magazine, edited by Péter Kuczka, was a special Philip K.
Dick issue. It contained Hungarian translations of all
but one of the stories in THE BOOK OF PHILIP K. DICK,
illustrated by Karakas András, plus an article on Dick
by Fazekas László, and five unrelated poems.

M29. THE HIGH CASTLE IN THE CELLAR
Commemorative Program Book for the First Annual Philip
K. Dick Conference, held at The Bookcellar Cafe in
Cambridge, MA on 25-Sep-1993.

M30. The New York Review of Science Fiction #70, 6-94 [K410,
K358, K243, K178, K118, K255, K389, K230,
K189]
Special Philip K. Dick issue of an American critical fanzine,
celebrating the First Annual Philip K. Dick Convention.

M31. PHILIP K. DICK: A CELEBRATION [G57, K364, O26, K86]
Program book for the event of the same name, held at Epping
Forest College, UK, 19/20-Oct-1991, and organized by Jeff
Merrifield and John Joyce as part of Connection (community
education) program.

M32. Portti 7-93 [A82, A103, A54, K11, K3]
Special Philip K. Dick issue of a Finnish SF magazine.

M33. Science Fiction Studies #5, 3-75 [K278, K388, K387, G35,
K289, K203, K41, K150, K244, K432, K269]
This was a special Philip K. Dick issue.
ON PHILIP K. DICK, Mullen/Csicsery-Ronay/Evans/Hollinger,
SF-TH Inc, 1992

M34. Science Fiction Studies #45, 7-88 [K154, K73, K151, K195,
K321, K131, K356, K334, K206, K56, K466, K130]
This was a special Philip K. Dick issue.
ON PHILIP K. DICK, Mullen/Csicsery-Ronay/Evans/Hollinger,
SF-TH Inc, 1992

M35. PHILIP K. DICK SOCIETY NEWSLETTERS (edited by Paul Williams)
For 10 years, from 1983 to 1992, Paul Williams ran the
Philip K. Dick Society, which published a total of 29
newsletters. No serious fan of Dick can afford to miss
these, because of the wealth of material included, and
most (if not all) are still available from Paul at
Box 611, GLEN ELLEN, CA 95442, UNITED STATES OF AMERICA.
The main contents of the 29 issues are as follows:

#0 (8-83) [G37]. Note that this was originally limited
     to 500 copies but has since been reprinted. This is
     labelled "PKDS Pamphlet #1".
#1 (8-83) [K452 and extracts from G17, L67, K345, K211]
#2 (12-83) [F32, K312, K113, L47, K453, K33]
#3 (4-84) [K219, K109, K197, K309, K342, G11, K5, K114,
     K59, A83, and extract from K377]
#4 (9-84) [F7, K313, K116, K339]
#5 (12-84) [K431, K160, and extract from G15]
#6 (4-85) [K103, K117, and extract from G15]
#7 (7-85) [K448, D11]
#8 (9-85) [A136, K325]
#9/10 (1-86) [J21]
#11 (5-86) [K66, G62, G58, K141, L56, L30, L55, L69,
     L42, L35, L58, and extracts from G59 & G61]
#12 (10-86) [G68, G60, G11, F38]
#13 (2-87) [D7, K324, G69, L6, L28]
#14 (6-87) [F21, F30]
#15 (8-87) [K212, F40, K331, K250, L37, L51, and extract
     from K260]
#16 (1-88) [A151, K472, L9, L39]
#17 (4-88) [F22, K12, K72, K115, L4, L71]
#18 (8-88) [F27, K449, K138, L40, L46]
#19 (1-89) [A85]
#20 (4-89) [K251, A130, K327, O14, K69, L12]
#21 (9-89) [K333]
#22/23 (12-89) [K385, K384, F23]
#24 (5-90) [F34, K458, F24, K13, K249, K328, K214]
#25 (12-90) [K436, K134, K349]
#26 (4-91) [K284, F16, K346]
#27 (8-91) [K446, F14]
#28 (3-92) [K221, A26, G13, K65, K364]
#29 (9-92) [O2, K400, K437, F41, F26, F11, K417, and
     extract from G17]
#30 (12-92) [G47, K110 + indexes to all issues]

M36. RADIO FREE P.K.D. edited by Greg Lee
This fanzine took over from the PHILIP K. DICK NEWSLETTERS
when the latter folded. Details are available from Greg at
27068 S. La Paz #430, ALISO VIEJO, CA 92656, UNITED STATES
OF AMERICA. Issues so far, together with their main
contents, are as follows:

#1 (2-93) [F39, K411, K457, K198]
#2 (5-93) [K241, K418, G48, K457]
#3 (10-93) [F34, K242, K239]
#4 (3-94) [K419, K207, O27, K163]

N. Phantom and Forthcoming Titles

N1. THE AMERASIAN TRILOGY
Proposed name for THE MAN IN THE HIGH CASTLE, THE SWASTIKA
AND THE CROSS, and FUJI IN WINTER.

N2. "The Day the Gods Stopped Laughing"
Unpublished, unfinished, article about philosophy, written
in the 1960s.

N3. THE DECKARD CHRONICLES by K.W. Jeter
A two-volume continuation of DO ANDROIDS DREAM OF ELECTRIC
SHEEP?, forthcoming from Orion (mentioned in Locus
#392, 9-93).

N4. "Dream by PKD Oct 2, 1960"
Unpublished article

N5. THE EARTHSHAKER
Projected novel written in 1948/49; only some opening
chapters and a detailed outline exist.

N6. THE EXEGESIS
1.5 million words of speculation on the philosophical and
theological meaning of life. Some extracts have been
published [G11, H1, H3].

N7. FIREBRIGHT: PKD: A LIFE 1962-1982 by Gregg Rickman
Projected second volume of biography, possibly to be split
into two volumes - CARDBOARD UNIVERSE: PKD: A LIFE
1962-1972 and FIREBRIGHT: PKD: A LIFE 1972-1982.

N8. THE FIRST LADY OF EARTH
    Phantom title listed in the Doubleday edition of
    THE THREE STIGMATA OF PALMER ELDRITCH.

N9. Foreign Language Items
    There are a number of foreign language items for which
    the corresponding English title is not known:

    Les Convertisseurs d'Armes {French}
      Galaxie #54, #55
    Dubleantan {Danish}
      Alt For Mænd 7-69

N10. FUJI IN WINTER
     Proposed sequel to THE MAN IN THE HIGH CASTLE and THE
     SWASTIKA AND THE CROSS.

N11. "A Good Savoyard is a Dead Savoyard"
     Unpublished article on Gilbert and Sulivan

   - THE GRASSHOPPER LIES HEAVY
     See under THE SWASTIKA AND THE CROSS

N12. IN THE MOLD OF YANCY
     Phantom title listed in the Doubleday edition of
     THE THREE STIGMATA OF PALMER ELDRITCH.

N13. JOE PROTAGORAS IS ALIVE AND LIVING ON EARTH
     Unwritten novel for which Dick submitted an outline in 1967.
     The outline was published in 1992 [see A60].

N14. A Little Girl and Snow
     Unpublished Poem

N15. A Man for No Countries
     Hypothetical story for a Philip Jose Farmer anthology.
     Later developed as RADIO FREE ALBEMUTH.

N16. Menace React
     Unpublished story fragment

N17. NICHOLAS AND THE HIGS
     Unpublished mainstream novel, written c. 1958, now lost.

N18. Operation Plowshare
    False title for `Project Plowshare' in Pyramid/Panther
    editions of THE ZAP GUN.

N19. THE OWL IN DAYLIGHT
    SF novel `in progress' when Dick died

N20. Phantom Editions
    Books in Print tends frequently to list spurious editions
    from Ultramarine (due presumably to over-optimistic
    forecasting on their part). Titles listed that do not
    appear in Christopher Stephens' definitive bibliography of
    Ultramarine (and hence must be considered phantom) include:
       DEUS IRAE (04527-1, -76, 182pp, $15)
       A SCANNER DARKLY (01613-1, -77, 220pp, $20)
       THE TRANSMIGRATION OF TIMOTHY ARCHER (44066-7, -82,
          255pp, $15)

    In addition, there is a phantom SFBC edition of SOLAR
    LOTTERY (77411, 188pp, $1.25) that is mentioned in some
    sources).

N21. PILGRIM ON THE HILL
    Unpublished mainstream novel, written c. 1956, now lost.

N22. RETURN TO LILLIPUT
    Novel based on Swift, written in 1942 at the age of 13.

  - RING OF FIRE {see under THE SWASTIKA AND THE CROSS}

N23. Robot `Kiss of Life' Drama in New Worlds #216, 9-79
    Credited to Dick in NEW WORLDS: AN ANTHOLOGY but actually
    by John T. Sladek.

N24. "School Talk for Drs. White and McNelly"
    Unpublished speech, delivered 7-73

N25. THE SEARCH FOR PHILIP K. DICK by Anne Dick
    Forthcoming biography

N26. THE SELECTED LETTERS OF PHILIP K. DICK: 1938-71 & 1980-82.
    Remaining two volumes of Dick's letters, forthcoming
    from Underwood-Miller.

N27. SELECTIONS FROM THE EXEGESIS: VOL II edited by Lawrence Sutin
Scheduled from Underwood-Miller for 9-92, but subsequently
cancelled.

N28. Sir Waldo and Sir Lunchalot
Story by `another author' accidentally included in the
Phil Dick manuscript collection at California State
University, Fullerton.

N29. The Song
Unpublished poem, written in 1940

N30. THE SWASTIKA AND THE CROSS
Proposed sequel to THE MAN IN THE HIGH CASTLE (outline only).
Also occasionally referred to as THE GRASSHOPPER LIES HEAVY
and as RING OF FIRE.

N31. `Teddy'
A number of stories and poems under the name `Teddy' have
been attributed to Dick after research done by Gregg
Rickman, and detailed in his biography of Dick [M17].
However, this attribution is disputed by other authorities,
so the items have not been listed in the main sections.
They are as follows:
    Autumn Mood (poem)
        The Berkeley Gazette 5-12-44
    Benediction (poem)
        The Berkeley Gazette 3-7-44
    The Clock Struck Thirteen (poem)
        The Berkeley Gazette 11-9-44
    Comments sent in by 'Teddy' (misc)
        The Berkeley Gazette 29-11-44
    Companions (poem)
        The Berkeley Gazette 6-11-44
    Crescent Romance (poem)
        The Berkeley Gazette 11-6-45
    Crunch! Crunch! (poem)
        The Berkeley Gazette 6-12-43
    Faust (poem)
        The Berkeley Gazette 19-2-45
    The Hope of Christmas (poem)
        The Berkeley Gazette 7-1-44
    How Can We Fail? (poem)
        The Berkeley Gazette 14-5-45
        TO THE HIGH CASTLE by Gregg Rickman, Fragments
            West, 1989
    Jet (poem)
        The Berkeley Gazette 28-2-44
    Knowledge (poem)
        The Berkeley Gazette 26-3-45

Motif (poem)
        The Berkeley Gazette 19-6-44
A Parable (poem)
        The Berkeley Gazette 27-11-44
The Past (poem)
        The Berkeley Gazette 20-11-44
        TO THE HIGH CASTLE by Gregg Rickman, Fragments
            West, 1989
Tomorrow is Another Day (sss)
        The Berkeley Gazette 2-7-45
Why Weep? (poem)
        The Berkeley Gazette 12-3-45

N32. THE THRASHER BASHERS
     Juvenile SF Novel for which Dick wrote an outline in 1962.

N33. A TIME FOR GEORGE STAVROS
     Early version of HUMPTY DUMPTY IN OAKLAND (c. 1956)

N34. Today the World
     Item in the Fullerton collection; content unknown.

N35. Untitled tribute to Frank Herbert
     Unpublished article

N36. VOICES FROM THE STREET
     547 page 'straight novel' written c. 1954.

N37. THE WHALE MOUTH COLONY
     Outline for novel, probably based on the second half of
            THE UNTELEPORTED MAN

N38. WORLDS OF SOUND AND COLOUR
     Full version of the interview by Gwen Lee & Doris E. Sauter
     [G23] planned for future publication.

O. Related Works by Other Authors

O1. KINDRED BLOOD IN KENSINGTON GORE by Brian W. Aldiss
            (dramatic dialogue for two)
        Presented {with Petronilla Whitfield} at Philip K. Dick: A
            Celebration, Epping Forest College, 19/20-Oct-1991.
        Avernus (ph) , 3-92, 25pp, £3.95 (?)

02. What Did the Policeman Say? In Memoriam for PKD by
        Brian W. Aldiss (poem)
    PKDS Newsletter (fnz) #29, 9-92

03. TOTAL RECALL by Piers Anthony [novelization of J28]
    Morrow (hb) 05209-6, 9-89, 246pp, $16.95 (John Berkey)
    Avon (pb) 70874-4, 6-90, 278pp, $4.50 (?) {slightly
        revised}
    Legend (hb) 3777-X, 7-90, 224pp, £12.99 (Tony Redhead)
    Legend (pb) 974200-4, 8-90, 224pp, £3.99 (Tony Redhead);
        10-90;

04. Welcome to Reality by Uwe Anton (ss)
    1974 {in German}
    WELCOME TO REALITY, Anton, Broken Mirrors Press, 1991
        {translated by Jim Young}

05. WELCOME TO REALITY: THE NIGHTMARES OF PHILIP K. DICK
            edited by Uwe Anton (anthology of stories
            influenced by Dick, about Dick, or featuring
            Dick as a character [C-14: K46, K444, O25, O16, O22,
            O4, O10, O7, O23, O20, O9, O11, O29, D11, O15, O21]
    Heyne (pb)   , 9-90   {in German} [contents differ,
        includes O13]
    Broken Mirrors Press (hb) 4-2, 1-91, 208pp, $55.00 (Dawn Wilson)
    Broken Mirrors Press (tp) 5-0, 1-91, 208pp, $12.95 (Wilson)

06. PHILIP K. DICK IS DEAD, ALAS by Michael Bishop (pastiche,
        featuring Dick as a character)
    Tor (hb) 93031-3, 10-87, 341pp, $16.95 (?) {as THE SECRET
        ASCENSION}
    Grafton (pb) 20151-3, 11-88, 411pp, £3.99 (Luis Rey)
    Tor (pb) 53157-4, 7-89, 341pp, $4.50 (?) {as THE SECRET
        ASCENSION}
    Orb (tp) 89002-8, 1-94, 341pp, $12.95 (Tom Canty)

07. Rogue Tomato by Michael Bishop (ss)
    NEW DIMENSIONS 5, Silverberg, Harper & Row, 1975
    BLOODED ON ARACHNE by Michael Bishop, Arkham House, 1982
    THE ROAD TO SCIENCE FICTION #4, Gunn, Mentor, 1982
    CHANGES, Bishop/Watson, Ace, 1983
    HUNGER FOR HORROR, Adams/Adams/Greenberg, DAW, 1988
    WELCOME TO REALITY, Anton, Broken Mirrors Press, 1991

08. Do Androids Dream by Jeni Couzyn (poem)
    HOUSE OF CHANGES by Jeni Couzyn, Heinemann, 1978

O9. The Girl with the Vita-Gel Hair by Thomas M. Disch
        (ss featurng Dick as a character)
    Omni 12-86
    WELCOME TO REALITY, Anton, Broken Mirrors Press, 1991

O10. A Man from the Future by Neil Ferguson (ss)
    Foundation #27, 2-83
    WELCOME TO REALITY, Anton, Broken Mirrors Press, 1991

O11. Philip K. Dick Is Dead and Living Happily in Wuppertal
            by Ronald M. Hahn (ss)
    1988 {in German}
    WELCOME TO REALITY, Anton, Broken Mirrors Press, 1991
            {translated by Jim Young}

O12. Untitled Poem by Noel K. Hannan (tribute to Dick)
    Sandor (fnz) #2, 1982

O13. Das PKD-Project by Michael Iwoleit (ss)
    Denebola #9, 1-90 {in German}
    WELCOME TO REALITY, Anton, Heyne, 1990 {in German}

O14. "The Riddle of TLE" by Eve La Plante (article about
            temporal lobe epilepsy)
    Atlantic 11-88
    PKDS Newsletter (fnz) #20, 4-89

O15. Agony and Remorse on Rhesus IX by Richard A. Lupoff (ss)
    Fantastic 8-72 {as by Ova Hamlet}
    THE OVA HAMLET PAPERS by Richard Lupoff, Pennyfarthing Press,
        1979
    WELCOME TO REALITY, Anton, Broken Mirrors Press, 1991

O16. The Digital Wristwatch of Philip K. Dick by Richard Lupoff (NT)
    THE DIGITAL WRISTWATCH OF PHILIP K. DICK by Richard Lupoff (1986)
    WELCOME TO REALITY, Anton, Broken Mirrors Press, 1991

O17. THE DIGITAL WRISTWATCH OF PHILIP K. DICK by Richard Lupoff [O16]
    Canyon Press, 1986
    Gryphon Books (tp) 25-7, 12-93, 28pp, $9.95 (Allen Koszowski)
        // HYPERPRISM

O18. Story by Achim Mehnert
    Denebola #9, 1-90 {in German}

019. Ocean of Glass and Fire by Rob Hollis Miller (short story
          about an attempt to deprogram a Phil Dick cultist)
     New Pathways #13, Winter 1988/89

020. Dick - A Gnostic Death in Life by Gero Reimann (NT)
     1984 {in German}
     WELCOME TO REALITY, Anton, Broken Mirrors Press, 1991
          {translated by Jim Young}

021. The Changeling by Robert Silverberg (ss)
     Amazing 11-82
     THE CONGLOMEROID COCKTAIL PARTY by Robert Silverberg,
          Arbor House, 1984
     WELCOME TO REALITY, Anton, Broken Mirrors Press, 1991

022. Solar Shoe-Salesman by John T. Sladek (parody)
     Fantasy and Science Fiction 3-73 {as by Chipdip K. Kill}
     THE STEAM-DRIVEN BOY, Sladek, Panther, 1973
     THE BEST OF JOHN SLADEK, Sladek, Pocket, 1981
     LIGHT YEARS AND DARK, Bishop, Berkley, 1984
     WELCOME TO REALITY, Anton, Broken Mirrors Press, 1991
          {as by Chipdip K. Kill}

023. Ubik Does the Trick by Norman Spinrad (poem)
     1983
     WELCOME TO REALITY, Anton, Broken Mirrors Press, 1991

024. Story by Joachim Stahl
     Denebola #9, 1-90 {in German}

025. The Transmigration of Philip K. by Michael Swanwick (ss)
     Isaac Asimov's SF Magazine 2-85
     WELCOME TO REALITY, Anton, Broken Mirrors Press, 1991

026. Four Scenes from Mutual Invasions, or the Book That Swallowed
          Philip K. Dick by Jim Thain {extracts from an
          unpublished novel, MUTUAL INVASIONS, OR THE BOOK
          THAT SWALLOWED PHILIP K. DICK, featuring Dick as
          a character, adapted as a play}
     PHILIP K. DICK: A CELEBRATION, Merrifield/Joyce,
          Connections, 1991

027. Wake-Up Call: An Excerpt from Mutual Invasions by Jim Thain
     Radio Free P.K.D. (fnz) #4, 3-94

028. Where the Wind Never Stops by Sam Umland (poem)
       PKDS Newsletter (fnz) #46, 4-91

029. A Little Something for Us Reincarnauts by Thomas Ziegler (NA)
       1989 {in German}
       WELCOME TO REALITY, Anton, Broken Mirrors Press, 1991
             {translated by Jim Young}

030. Winners of the Philip K. Dick Award
       1983: SOFTWARE by Rudy Rucker
       1984: THE ANUBIS GATES by Tim Powers
       1985: NEUROMANCER by William Gibson
       1986: DINNER AT DEVIANT'S PALACE by Tim Powers
       1987: HOMUNCULUS by James Blaylock
       1988: STRANGE TOYS by Patricia Geary
       1989: 400 BILLION STARS by Paul J. McAuley
             WETWARE by Rudy Rucker
       1990: SUBTERRANEAN GALLERY by Richard Paul Russo
       1991: POINTS OF DEPARTURE by Pat Murphy
       1992: KING OF MORNING, QUEEN OF DAY by Ian McDonald
       1993: THROUGH THE HEART by Richard Grant
       1994: GROWING UP WEIGHTLESS by John M. Ford
             ELVISSEY by Jack Womack

P. Textual Variations

P1. A. Lincoln, Simulacrum / WE CAN BUILD YOU
       When 'A. Lincoln Simulacrum' was submitted to Amazing,
       Ted White commented that it had no ending and suggested
       that Dick should write one. Dick asked White to draft
       something he thought suitable. Ted White wrote a 3,000
       word ending and sent it to Dick for comment. Dick changed
       only three words and it was published as such. When the
       book edition was published, Dick insisted that the ending
       be omitted.

P2. SOLAR LOTTERY / WORLD OF CHANCE
       Apparently the first draft, under the title QUIZMASTER
       TAKES ALL, was 63,000 words long. Dick revised this to
       60,000 words for Don Wollheim at Ace, who published it as
       SOLAR LOTTERY. Meanwhile, the original manuscript was
       sent to Rich & Cowan who edited it (badly) and published
       it as WORLD OF CHANCE. For more details see Gregg
       Rickman's article [K333] in PKDS Newsletter #21, 9-89.

P3. THE UNTELEPORTED MAN / LIES, INC.
This was first published in a magazine in 1964. In 1966
Dick wrote a further 30,000 words but they weren't used
and the initial book edition (Ace 1966) was identical
to the magazine edition.

Much later Dick arranged for the publication in the USA
of a complete edition, with extensive revisions. However,
he died before completion and the revisions could not be
found, so the Berkley (1983) edition published the full
1966 version, with gaps in the text where four manuscript
pages had gone missing during the long years in storage.

Then, in November 1983, Dick's literary executor found the
revised and retitled typescript, which was published for
the first time by Gollancz with the two remaining gaps (of
1 page each) completed by John Sladek.

The remaining missing pages were found by Paul Williams in
1985, and were published in PKDS Newsletter (fnz) #8, 9-85.

Q. Chronological Listing of Fiction
Note that this listing is primarily in order of date of
submission (first column), based on the information in
THE COLLECTED STORIES OF PHILIP K. DICK. Where a date of
submission is not known, the date of publication is used
(second column).

1942
23-1-42	Le Diable
5-2-42	The Handy Puddle
17-2-42	Jungle People
16-9-42	The Black Box
7-10-42	The Pirate
27-10-42	Knight Fight!

1943
30-8-43	Stratosphere Betsy
26-10-43	The Highbrow

1944
4-1-44	Santa's Return
7-2-44	The Magician's Box
8-5-44	The Slave Race
22-5-44	The First Presentation
14-8-44	The Visitation

```
1947
    ??-47      5-87   Stability


1951
    11-51      2-53   Roog


1952
               7-52   Beyond Lies the Wub
    23-7-52    12-53  The Builder
    24-7-52    10-54  Meddler
    31-7-52    6-53   Paycheck
    31-7-52    8-53   Out in the Garden
    31-7-52    12-53  The Great C
     4-8-52    9-53   The King of the Elves
    11-8-52    6-53   Colony
    14-8-52    Win54  Prize Ship
    26-8-52    Spr55  Nanny
    27-8-52    6-53   The Cookie Lady
    29-8-52    1-54   Beyond the Door
               9-52   The Gun
               9-52   The Skull
     3-10-52   5-53   Second Variety
    21-10-52   ??-54  Jon's World
    22-10-52   7-53   The Cosmic Poachers
               11-52  The Little Movement
     3-11-52   10-53  Some Kinds of Life
     3-11-52   11-54  Progeny
     5-11-52   6-53   Martians Come in Clouds
    19-11-52   8-53   The Commuter
    24-11-52   5-53   The World She Wanted
     2-12-52   7-55   A Surface Raid
      ??-52    6-94   GATHER YOURSELVES TOGETHER


1953
               1-53   Mr. Spaceship
               1-53   The Defenders
     6-1-53    12-53  Project: Earth
    13-1-53    9-53   The Trouble with Bubbles
    17-1-53    1-54   A Present for Pat
    17-1-53    7-54   Breakfast at Twilight
    26-1-53    7-54   Of Withered Apples
    26-1-53    6-55   The Hood Maker
               2-53   Piper in the Woods
     2-2-53    Win55  Human Is
    11-2-53    10-53  The Impossible Planet
    11-2-53    9-54   Adjustment Team
    24-2-53    6-53   Impostor
    17-3-53    5-54   James P. Crow
    23-3-53    10-53  Planet for Transients
    23-3-53    5-54   Small Town
    26-3-53    10-54  Souvenir
```

Philip K. Dick - 149

```
1953 (cont)
     3-4-53     5-54    Survey Team
    16-4-53     2-56    Vulcan's Hammer
    20-4-53     5-54    Prominent Author
    21-4-53     9-59    Fair Game
               5-53    The Infinites
     4-5-53    12-53    The Hanging Stranger
    13-5-53    Sum53    The Eyes Have It
               6-53    The Preserving Machine
     5-6-53    Sum54    Time Pawn
    24-6-53     4-54    The Golden Man
               7-53    Expendable
               7-53    The Indefatigable Frog
     8-7-53    Sum54    The Turning Wheel
    15-7-53    11-54    The Last of the Masters
    21-7-53    12-54    The Father-Thing
     4-8-53    12-54    Strange Eden
    19-8-53    12-56    A Glass of Darkness
    31-8-53    Spr54    Tony and the Beetles
    31-8-53    12-58    Null-O
               9-53    The Variable Man
    21-10-53    8-54    Exhibit Piece
    21-10-53    2-56    To Serve the Master
    29-10-53    7-54    The Crawlers
    19-11-53    6-54    Sales Pitch
    22-12-53    9-54    Shell Game
    30-12-53   11-54    Upon the Dull Earth
    31-12-53    1-55    Foster, You're Dead!


1954
               1-54    The Crystal Crypt
               1-54    The Short Happy Life of the Brown Oxford
    28-1-54    10-56    Pay for the Printer
    17-2-54     3-55    War Veteran
     9-4-54     7-55    The Chromium Fence
    14-5-54     2-57    Misadjustment
     4-6-54    10-54    A World of Talent
     8-6-54    11-55    Psi-Man Heal My Child!
    11-10-54    7-55    Service Call
    11-10-54   11-55    Autofac
    18-10-54    4-55    Captive Market
    18-10-54    8-55    The Mold of Yancy
    13-12-54    3-56    THE WORLD JONES MADE
    21-12-54    5-55    SOLAR LOTTERY
    22-12-54    1-56    The Minority Report


1955
    15-2-55    ??-57    EYE IN THE SKY
     2-6-55     1-57    The Unreconstructed M
               8-55    A HANDFUL OF DARKNESS
    17-10-55   12-56    THE MAN WHO JAPED
    ??-55       3-87    MARY AND THE GIANT
```

```
1956
   13-11-56     7-88   THE BROKEN BUBBLE


1957
    1-5-57     10-57   THE COSMIC PUPPETS
   15-5-57     10-85   PUTTERING ABOUT IN A SMALL LAND
     ??-57     ??-57   THE VARIABLE MAN AND OTHER STORIES


1958
    7-4-58     ??-59   TIME OUT OF JOINT
    2-5-58      7-59   Recall Mechanism
    6-5-58      1-59   Explorers We
    8-10-58     6-85   IN MILTON LUMKY TERRITORY
   31-10-58    12-59   War Game


1959
   28-7-59      2-60   DR. FUTURITY
     ??-59     ??-75   CONFESSIONS OF A CRAP ARTIST


1960
   16-2-60      9-60   VULCAN'S HAMMER
   10-5-60      6-84   THE MAN WHOSE TEETH WERE ALL EXACTLY ALIKE
   10-60      10-86   HUMPTY DUMPTY IN OAKLAND


1961
   29-11-61    10-62   THE MAN IN THE HIGH CASTLE


1962
    4-10-62     1-70   A. Lincoln, Simulacrum
    4-10-62     7-72   WE CAN BUILD YOU
   31-10-62     4-64   MARTIAN TIME-SLIP


1963
   11-2-63      6-65   DR. BLOODMONEY OR HOW WE GOT ALONG AFTER
                       THE BOMB
   27-2-63     12-63   If There Were No Benny Cemoli
   23-3-63      2-64   Novelty Act
   10-4-63      1-64   Waterspider
   15-4-63      6-64   What the Dead Men Say
   16-4-63     ??-64   Orpheus with Clay Feet
   18-4-63     10-63   Stand-By
   29-4-63     11-63   What'll We Do with Ragland Park?
    6-5-63      2-64   Oh, To Be A Blobel!
    6-5-63      8-64   The Little Black Box
    4-6-63     12-63   THE GAME-PLAYERS OF TITAN
   28-8-63     ??-64   THE SIMULACRA
    9-9-63      7-64   Cantata 140
```

```
1963 (cont)
                12-63   All we Marsmen
                12-63   The Days of Perky Pat
      4-12-63   5-66    NOW WAIT FOR LAST YEAR
      5-12-63   1-88    The Zap Gun (outline)
      9-12-63   7-64    A Game of Unchance
      9-12-63   10-64   Precious Artifact
     23-12-63   1-65    Retreat Syndrome
        ??-63   4-89    Today the World


1964
      16-1-64   11-64   CLANS OF THE ALPHANE MOON
      17-3-64   2-66    THE CRACK IN SPACE
      18-3-64   11-64   THE THREE STIGMATA OF PALMER ELDRITCH
                Spr64   The War with the Fnools
      15-4-64   1-67    THE ZAP GUN
      12-5-64   9-64    THE PENULTIMATE TRUTH
      26-8-64   12-64   The Unteleported Man
      26-8-64   11-66   THE UNTELEPORTED MAN


1965
       5-5-65   9-85    THE UNTELEPORTED MAN (2 missing pages)
      27-8-65   8-66    Your Appointment Will Be Yesterday
      13-9-65   4-66    We Can Remember It For You Wholesale
      13-9-65   5-66    Holy Quarrel
      21-9-65   Sum68   Not By Its Cover
     14-10-65   2-67    Return Match
        ??-65   2-67    COUNTER-CLOCK WORLD


1966
                1-66    Project Plowshare
      17-1-66   10-67   Faith of Our Fathers
      16-8-66   6-67    THE GANYMEDE TAKEOVER
      20-6-66   3-68    DO ANDROIDS DREAM OF ELECTRIC SHEEP?
      7-12-66   5-69    UBIK
      7-12-66   6-88    NICK AND THE GLIMMUNG


1967
       4-5-67   8-92    The Name of the Game is Death
        ??-67   8-92    Joe Protagoras is Alive and Living on Earth


1968
        3-68    5-69    GALACTIC POT-HEALER
                Fal68   The Story to End All Stories for Harlan
                          Ellison's Anthology DANGEROUS VISIONS
     31-10-68   7-70    A MAZE OF DEATH
      6-11-88   1-89    Our Friends From Frolix 8 (outline)
      4-12-68   10-69   The Electric Ant
```

```
1969
                4-69   THE PRESERVING MACHINE AND OTHER STORIES
      2-7-69    6-70   OUR FRIENDS FROM FROLIX 8


1970
               10-70   A PHILIP K. DICK OMNIBUS


1971
      12-71    ??-7?   Cadbury, the Beaver Who Lacked


1973
                2-73   THE BOOK OF PHILIP K. DICK
    13-2-73     ??-74  A Little Something for Us Tempunaut
    20-12-73   10-74   The Pre-Persons


1974
               ??-74   FLOW MY TEARS, THE POLICEMAN SAID


1975
    15-5-75     3-87   The Eye of the Sibyl
    17-8-75     7-76   DEUS IRAE
    29-8-75    ??-77   A SCANNER DARKLY


1976
    19-8-76    12-85   RADIO FREE ALBEMUTH


1977
                3-77   THE BEST OF PHILIP K DICK
      Sum77     5-87   The Day Mr. Computer Fell out of its Tree


1978
    7-12-78     2-81   VALIS


1979
    21-6-79    Fal79   The Exit Door Leads In
     9-7-79     5-80   Chains of Air, Web of Aether


1980
                2-80   THE GOLDEN MAN
    27-3-80    Sum84   Strange Memories of Death
    24-4-80    12-80   I Hope I Shall Arrive Soon
    13-5-80    10-80   Rautavaara's Case
      6-80      6-81   THE DIVINE INVASION
     4-8-80     8-87   Fawn, Look Back
    17-11-80   12-89   11-17-80
```

```
1981
                2-81   The Alien Mind
    13-5-81     4-82   THE TRANSMIGRATION OF TIMOTHY ARCHER


1984
    17-3-84     5-87   A Terran Odyssey
                4-84   Once There Was an Ant
                6-84   ROBOTS, ANDROIDS, AND MECHANICAL ODDITIES


1985
                7-85   I HOPE I SHALL ARRIVE SOON


1987
                5-87   BEYOND LIES THE WUB
                5-87   SECOND VARIETY
                5-87   THE FATHER-THING
                5-87   THE DAYS OF PERKY PAT
                5-87   THE LITTLE BLACK BOX


1988
                12-88  Goodbye, Vincent


1989
                12-89  THE VALIS TRILOGY


1992           3-92   The Different Stages of Love
```